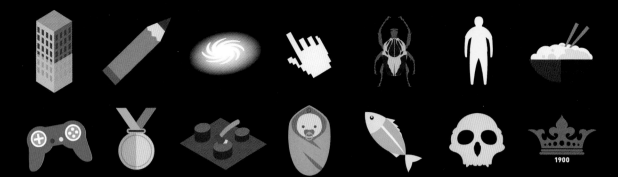

ATLAS OF
EVERY
THING

Maps that help you make sense of the world

WAYLAND

First published in Great Britain in 2015 by Wayland
The edition published in 2016

Copyright © Wayland 2015

The material in this book has previously been published in the
following titles: *Mapographica: Art, Culture and Sport, Mapographica: People on Earth,
Mapographica: The Manmade World* and *Mapographica: The Natural World.*

Original series produced by Tall Tree Ltd
Interior Design: Alyssa Peacock
Cover Design: Simon Letchford
Editorial Consultant: Hayley Fairhead
Editor: Corinne Lucas

ISBN 978 0 7502 9880 3

MIX
Paper from
responsible sources
FSC
www.fsc.org   FSC® C104740

10 9 8 7 6 5 4 3 2

Wayland, an imprint of
Hachette Children's Group
Part of Hodder and Stoughton
Carmelite House
50 Victoria Embankment
London EC4Y 0DZ

An Hachette UK Company

www.hachette.co.uk
www.hachettechildrens.co.uk

Printed and bound in Italy by L.E.G.O. S.p.A.

Picture credits can be found on page 112.

CONTENTS

The World in
100 PEOPLE

If you reduced the world's population to just 100 people, then an 'average' person would live in a town in Asia, speak Chinese and be between 15 and 64 years old. They would not have a college degree, own a computer, use social media or the internet. However, they would be able to read and write, own a mobile phone, have access to electricity and safe water, and they would be living on more than US$2 a day.

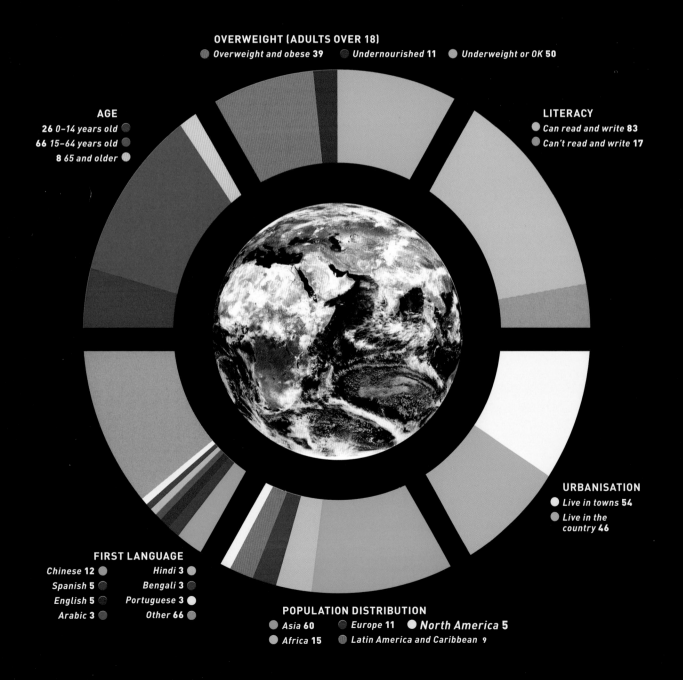

OVERWEIGHT (ADULTS OVER 18)
Overweight and obese 39   Undernourished 11   Underweight or OK 50

AGE
26 0–14 years old
66 15–64 years old
8 65 and older

LITERACY
Can read and write 83
Can't read and write 17

URBANISATION
Live in towns 54
Live in the country 46

FIRST LANGUAGE
Chinese 12   Hindi 3
Spanish 5   Bengali 3
English 5   Portuguese 3
Arabic 3   Other 66

POPULATION DISTRIBUTION
Asia 60   Europe 11   North America 5
Africa 15   Latin America and Caribbean 9

Our
PLANET

The world is divided into large landmasses, called continents, and together these cover 148.94 million sq km, which is a little under 30 per cent of Earth's total surface area. The continents feature towering peaks that stretch high into the atmosphere, rivers that wind for thousands of kilometres and vast islands.

EUROPE

NORTH AMERICA

ASIA

AFRICA

SOUTH AMERICA

OCEANIA

NORTH AMERICA

Highest mountains

Denali
6,194 m

Mt Logan
5,959 m

Pico de Orizaba
5,636 m

Longest rivers

Missouri 3,767 km

Mississippi 3,734 km

Yukon 3,187 km

Largest islands

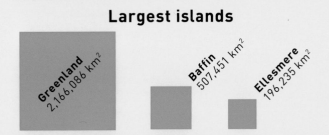

Greenland
2,166,086 km²

Baffin
507,451 km²

Ellesmere
196,235 km²

SOUTH AMERICA

Highest mountains

Aconcagua
6,995 m

Oyos del Salado
6,893 m

Pississ
6,793 m

Longest rivers

Amazon 6,437 km

Paraná 4,880 km

Madeira 3,250 km

Largest islands

Isla Grande de Tierra del Fuego
248,000 km²

Marajó
40,100 km²

Chiloé
8,394 km²

EUROPE

Highest mountains

Elbrus 5,642 m
Kazbek 5,033 m
Mont Blanc 4,810 m

Longest rivers

Volga 3,692 km

Danube 2,860 km

Ural 2,428 km

Largest islands

Great Britain 229,885 km²
Iceland 102,775 km²
Ireland 84,421 km²

AFRICA

Highest mountains

Kilimanjaro 5,895 m
Kenya 5,199 m
Mawenzi 5,149 m

Longest rivers

Nile 6,853 km

Congo 4,700 km

Niger 4,180 km

Largest islands

Madagascar 587,000 km²
Socotra 3,796 km²
Réunion 969 km²

ASIA

Highest mountains

Mt Everest 8,850 m
K2 8,611 m
Kanchenjunga 8,586 m

Longest rivers

Yangtze 6,300 km

Yellow 5,464 km

Lena 4,400 km

Largest islands

Borneo 743,330 km²
Sumatra 473,481 km²
Honshu 227,898 km²

7

OCEANIA

Highest mountains

Wilheim 4,509 m
Giluwe 4,367 m
Mauna-Kea 4,205 m

Longest rivers

Murray 2,375 km

Murrumbidgee 1,485 km

Darling 1,472 km

Largest islands

New Guinea 462,840 km²
New Zealand South island 151,215 km²
New Zealand North island 113,729 km²

DESERTS

A desert is a region that receives less than 25 centimetres of precipitation each year. Deserts cover about one-third of Earth's land area and they can be hot or cold. They are covered in sand, rocky scrub or ice sheets.

MAJOR DESERTS

Great Basin
North America
490,000 km²

8

7

Chihuahuan
Mexico,
453,000 km²

9

**GREAT DUNE OF PYLA,
ARCACHON BAY**
France
107m
Tallest sand dune in Europe

**ISAOUANE-N-TIFERNINE
SAND SEA**
Algeria
430m
Tallest sand dunes in Africa

Sahara
Africa
9,100,000 km²

**DUNA FEDERICO
KIRBUS**
Argentina
1,230m
*Tallest sand dune
in the world*

5

Patagonian
South America,
670,000 km²

KEY

Major Deserts
The world's major deserts and their sizes

Danger of desertification
These regions are usually found next to existing deserts and may become deserts themselves.

Tallest sand dunes
Dunes are created when wind blows over large areas of sand, creating waves, or dunes, some of which can be hundreds of metres tall.

Singing Sand

'Singing Sand' can sometimes be heard in a desert when a surface layer of sand flows down a dune, perhaps disturbed by someone walking near the top. The noise can be a low boom or a shrill squeak with a volume of up to 105 decibels – as loud as a revving snowmobile engine.

Syrian
Arabian Peninsula
490,000 km²

Gobi
China and Mongolia
1,300,000 km²

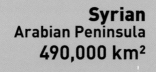

8

4

9

BADAIN JARAN DUNES
China
500m
Tallest sand dunes in Asia

2

3

Arabian
Arabian Peninsula
2,600,000 km²

Great Victoria
Australia
647,000 km²

6

7

Kalahari
Africa
570,000 km²

Antarctic
Antarctica
14,200,000 km²

MOUNT TEMPEST, MORETON ISLAND
Australia
285m
Tallest coastal sand dune

1

OCEANS

Earth's oceans are vast, and we have only explored less than 5 per cent of them. Beneath the surface are thousands of undiscovered species, as well as physical features such as volcanoes, canyons and mountain ridges.

THE WORLD'S OCEANS

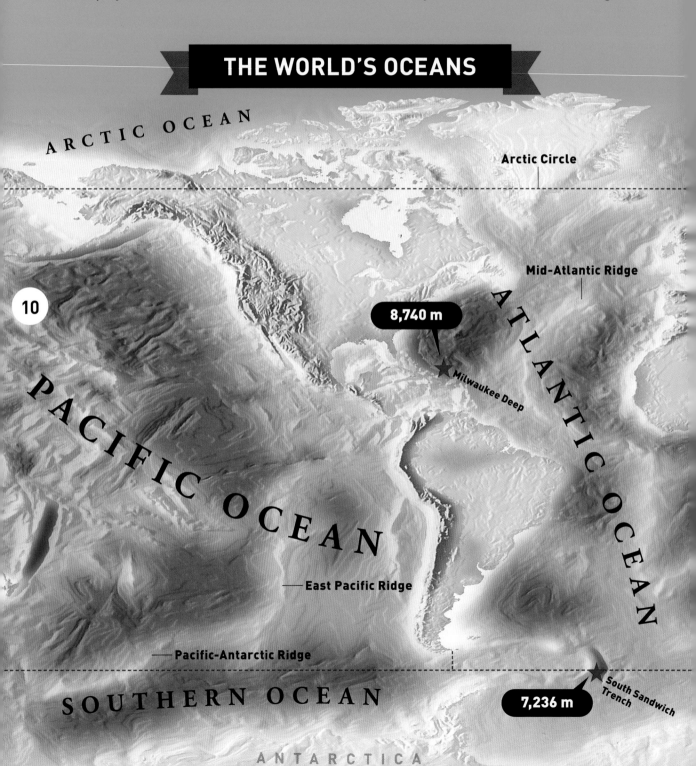

ARCTIC OCEAN

Arctic Circle

Mid-Atlantic Ridge

8,740 m

★ Milwaukee Deep

ATLANTIC OCEAN

10

PACIFIC OCEAN

—— East Pacific Ridge

—— Pacific-Antarctic Ridge

SOUTHERN OCEAN

7,236 m ★ South Sandwich Trench

ANTARCTICA

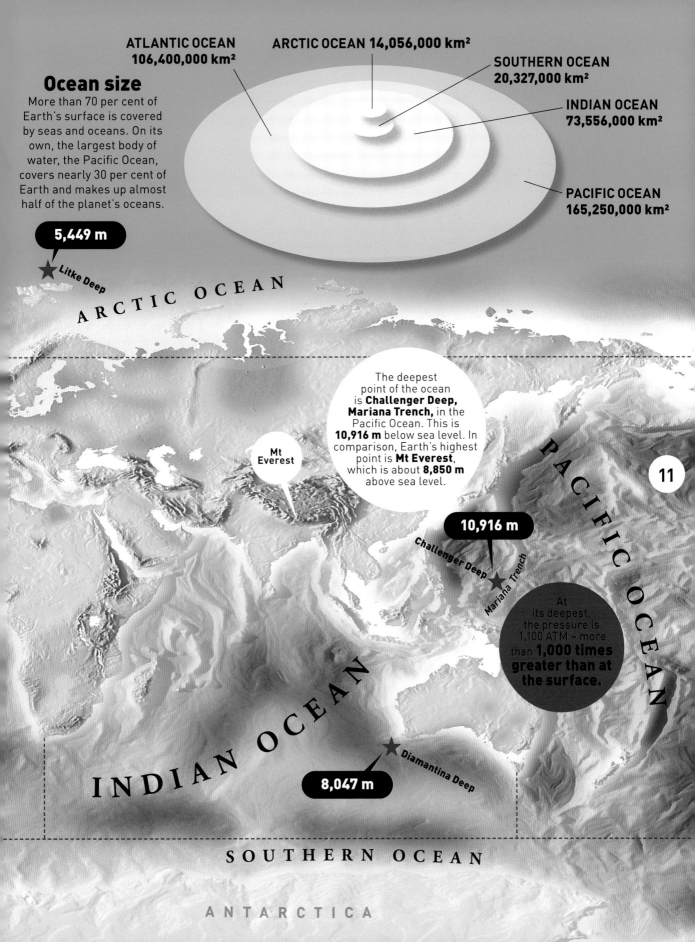

Ocean size

More than 70 per cent of Earth's surface is covered by seas and oceans. On its own, the largest body of water, the Pacific Ocean, covers nearly 30 per cent of Earth and makes up almost half of the planet's oceans.

ATLANTIC OCEAN 106,400,000 km²

ARCTIC OCEAN 14,056,000 km²

SOUTHERN OCEAN 20,327,000 km²

INDIAN OCEAN 73,556,000 km²

PACIFIC OCEAN 165,250,000 km²

5,449 m

★ Litke Deep

ARCTIC OCEAN

The deepest point of the ocean is **Challenger Deep, Mariana Trench,** in the Pacific Ocean. This is **10,916 m** below sea level. In comparison, Earth's highest point is **Mt Everest,** which is about **8,850 m** above sea level.

Mt Everest

PACIFIC OCEAN

10,916 m

Challenger Deep ★ Mariana Trench

At its deepest, the pressure is 1,100 ATM – more than **1,000 times greater than at the surface.**

INDIAN OCEAN

★ Diamantina Deep

8,047 m

SOUTHERN OCEAN

ANTARCTICA

Plates and QUAKES

Earth's crust is split up into huge blocks, called tectonic plates. These move about slowly, crashing into each other, scraping together or pulling apart, triggering powerful earthquakes with devastating effects.

TECTONIC PLATES

This map shows the world's tectonic plates, the direction in which they are moving and the locations of the most powerful and deadliest earthquakes.

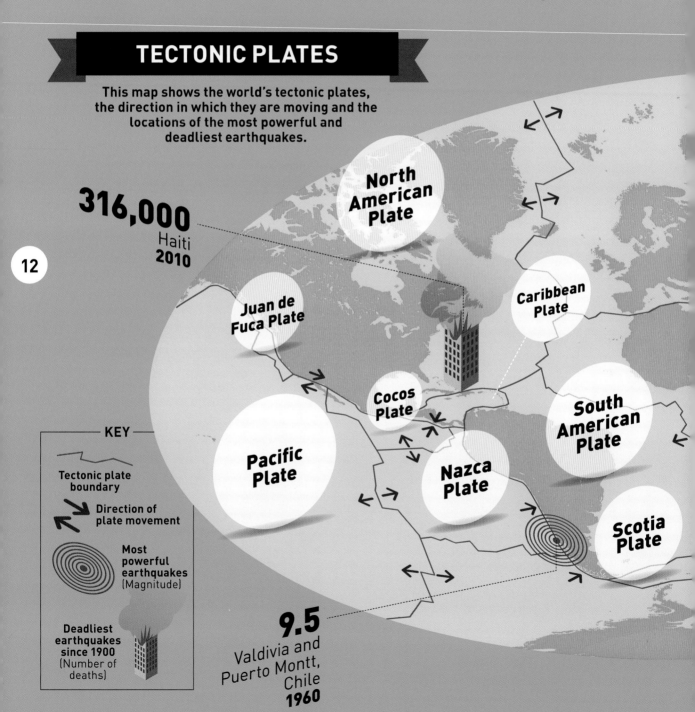

316,000
Haiti
2010

North American Plate

Caribbean Plate

Juan de Fuca Plate

Cocos Plate

South American Plate

Pacific Plate

Nazca Plate

Scotia Plate

KEY

Tectonic plate boundary

Direction of plate movement

Most powerful earthquakes (Magnitude)

Deadliest earthquakes since 1900 (Number of deaths)

9.5
Valdivia and Puerto Montt, Chile
1960

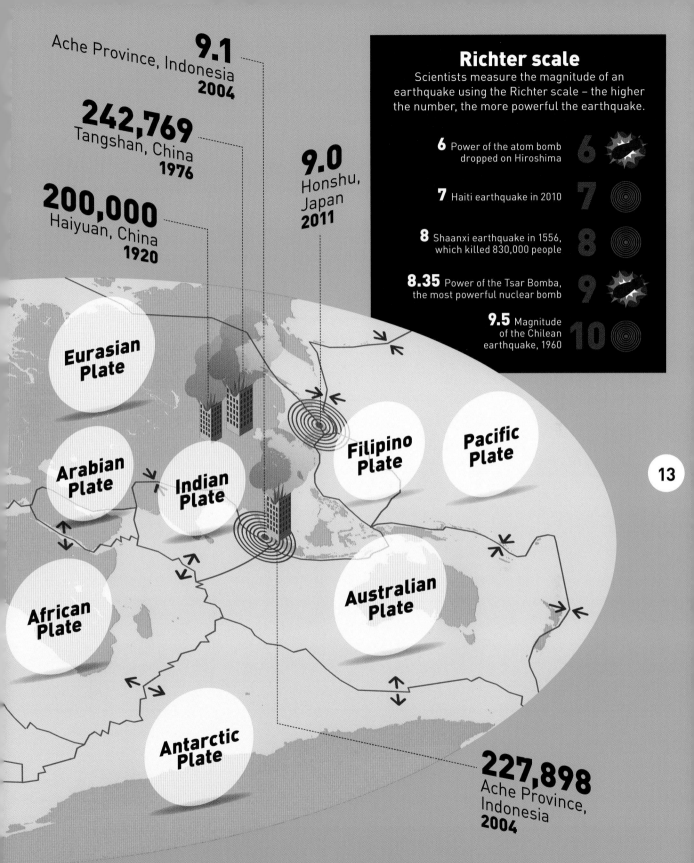

9.1
Ache Province, Indonesia
2004

242,769
Tangshan, China
1976

200,000
Haiyuan, China
1920

9.0
Honshu,
Japan
2011

13

Eurasian Plate

Arabian Plate

Indian Plate

Filipino Plate

Pacific Plate

African Plate

Australian Plate

Antarctic Plate

227,898
Ache Province,
Indonesia
2004

The Indonesian earthquake of 2004 created a huge wave, or **tsunami**, that destroyed many coastal areas in the region.

VOLCANOES

Volcanoes are holes in the Earth's crust through which super-hot molten rock, or lava, pours out of the ground. Most of them are found around the edges of Earth's tectonic plates, but some are found in the middle of a plate, where the rock is thin enough for lava to erupt.

ACTIVE VOLCANOES

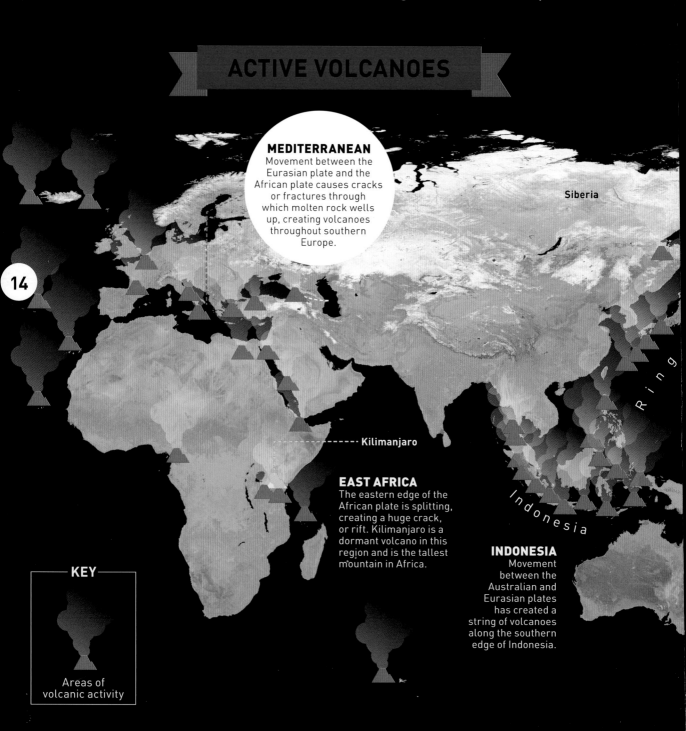

MEDITERRANEAN
Movement between the Eurasian plate and the African plate causes cracks or fractures through which molten rock wells up, creating volcanoes throughout southern Europe.

Siberia

Ring

Indonesia

- - - - - Kilimanjaro

EAST AFRICA
The eastern edge of the African plate is splitting, creating a huge crack, or rift. Kilimanjaro is a dormant volcano in this region and is the tallest mountain in Africa.

INDONESIA
Movement between the Australian and Eurasian plates has created a string of volcanoes along the southern edge of Indonesia.

KEY

Areas of volcanic activity

DIFFERENT TYPES OF VOLCANO

Caldera
A large crater or bowl that is formed when land collapses during an eruption.

Shield
Formed by runny lava, which hardens to create a large volcano with a low profile.

Dome
Formed by thick lava, which hardens to create a circular mound.

Composite
Also known as a stratovolcano, this is formed by layers of lava, rock and ash that build up over successive eruptions.

YELLOWSTONE
Beneath the Yellowstone National Park is one of the biggest volcanoes on the planet. This supervolcano last erupted more than 600,000 years ago.

ALASKA
Tectonic activity in the northern Pacific has created a string of volcanoes that stretch from Alaska to Siberia.

of Fire

15

EASTERN PACIFIC
The ring of volcanoes around the Pacific Ocean is known as the Pacific Ring of Fire. The eastern edge of this ring is created by movement between the Pacific, Filipino and North American plates.

Yellowstone Park

HAWAII
The Hawaiian volcanoes are found in the middle of the Pacific Plate, far away from any plate boundaries. Here, the plate is so thin that it creates a hotspot where volcanoes are formed.

There are more than
1,500
active volcanoes around the world. An active volcano is one that has erupted in the last 10,000 years.

New Zealand

ANDES
The volcanoes of the Andes are formed by the Nazca Plate being pushed beneath the South American Plate as the two crash into each other.

Natural
DISASTERS

Regular seasonal extremes of rainfall and temperature create severe storms that lash regions and cause huge amounts of damage. Other deadly disasters include avalanches and huge earthquake-created tsunamis.

THE WORST DISASTERS

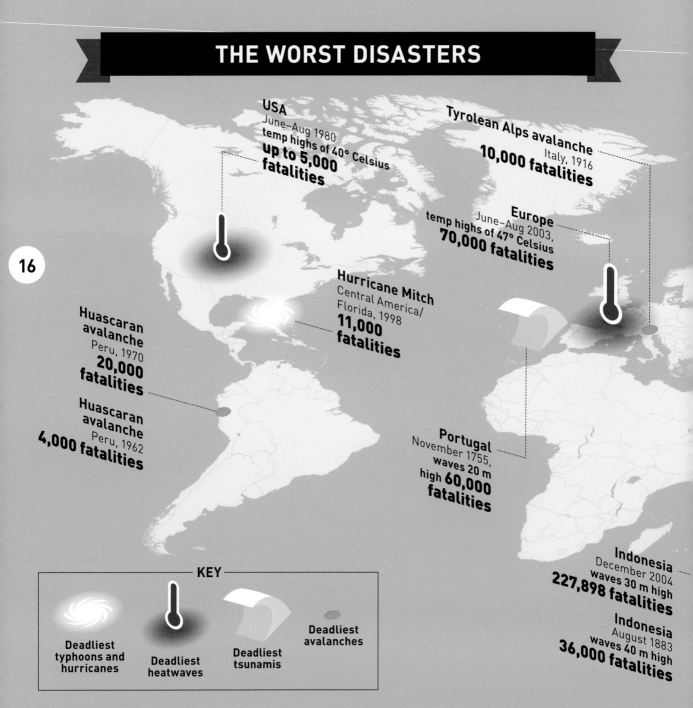

USA
June–Aug 1980
temp highs of 40° Celsius
up to 5,000 fatalities

Tyrolean Alps avalanche
Italy, 1916
10,000 fatalities

Europe
June–Aug 2003,
temp highs of 47° Celsius
70,000 fatalities

Hurricane Mitch
Central America/
Florida, 1998
11,000 fatalities

Huascaran avalanche
Peru, 1970
20,000 fatalities

Huascaran avalanche
Peru, 1962
4,000 fatalities

Portugal
November 1755,
waves 20 m
high **60,000 fatalities**

Indonesia
December 2004
waves 30 m high
227,898 fatalities

Indonesia
August 1883
waves 40 m high
36,000 fatalities

KEY

Deadliest typhoons and hurricanes

Deadliest heatwaves

Deadliest tsunamis

Deadliest avalanches

16

Deadly events

As well as the four events shown here, natural disasters can include earthquakes and volcanic eruptions, floods, blizzards, droughts, tornadoes, wildfires and even meteorite impacts.

Typhoons and Hurricanes
Massive swirling storms called cyclones, typhoons or hurricanes can measure hundreds of kilometres across.

Heatwaves
Prolonged periods of high temperatures are called heatwaves. They can trigger fires and can be dangerous to vulnerable people, such as the elderly and very young.

Avalanches
Huge slides of snow that crash down mountain slopes are known as avalanches. They can travel at speeds of up to 400 km/h.

Tsunamis
These are enormous waves that are usually triggered by earthquakes and underwater volcanic eruptions. These waves rush ashore and destroy everything in their path, before sweeping back out to sea.

Russia
July–Sept 2010
temp highs of 44° Celsius
56,000 fatalities

India
May–June 2003,
temp highs of 47° Celsius
1,500 fatalities

Bhola Cyclone
Bangladesh, 1970
500,000 fatalities

Bangladesh Cyclone
Bangladesh, 1991
138,366 fatalities

Japan
July–Sept 2010
temp highs of 35° Celsius
1,718 fatalities

Super Typhoon Nina
China, 1975
229,000 fatalities

Cyclone Nargis
Myanmar, 2008
138,366 fatalities

Japan September 1498
waves estimated 10–20 m
31,000 fatalities

Japan
March 2011
waves 10 m high
18,000 fatalities

17

Human
WORLD

The world is divided into large landmasses, called continents. The 7.4 billion people who live on the planet are not scattered evenly across these continents – more than 60 per cent of these people live in just one continent, Asia.

EUROPE

NORTH AMERICA

ASIA

AFRICA

SOUTH AMERICA

OCEANIA

NORTH AMERICA

Number of countries

●●●●●●●●●●●●●●●●
●●●●●●●●●● **26**

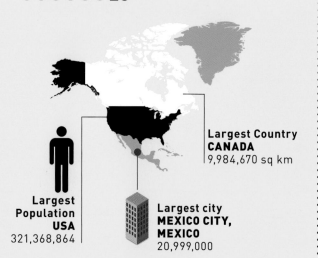

Largest Population USA
321,368,864

Largest Country CANADA
9,984,670 sq km

Largest city MEXICO CITY, MEXICO
20,999,000

Total Area
24,709,000 sq km

Total Population
364 million

SOUTH AMERICA

Number of countries

●●●●●●●●●●●●●●●● **16**

Largest Country BRAZIL
8,514,877 sq km

Largest Population BRAZIL
204,259,812

Largest city SAO PAULO, BRAZIL
21,066,000

Total Area
17,840,000 sq km

Total Population
419 million

EUROPE

Number of countries

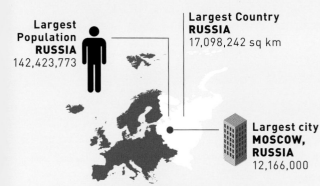

47

Largest Population
RUSSIA
142,423,773

Largest Country
RUSSIA
17,098,242 sq km

Largest city
MOSCOW, RUSSIA
12,166,000

Total Area
10,180,000 sq km

Total Population
743 million

ASIA

Number of countries

52

Largest Population
CHINA
1,367,485,388

Largest Country
RUSSIA (Asia)
17,098,242 sq km

Largest city
TOKYO, JAPAN
38,001,000

Total Area
44,579,000 sq km

Total Population
4.43 billion

AFRICA

Number of countries

●●●●●●●●●●●●●●●●●●●●
●●●●●●●●●●●●●●●●●●●
●●●●●●●●●●●●●●●●●●● 57

Largest Country
ALGERIA
2,381,741 sq km

Largest city
LAGOS, NIGERIA
13,123,000

Largest Population
NIGERIA
181,562,056

Total Area
30,221,532 sq km

Total Population
1.2 billion

OCEANIA

Number of countries

●●●●●●●●●●●●●●●●●●● 19

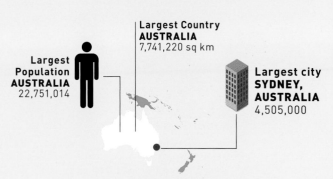

Largest Population
AUSTRALIA
22,751,014

Largest Country
AUSTRALIA
7,741,220 sq km

Largest city
SYDNEY, AUSTRALIA
4,505,000

Total Area
8,525,989 sq km

Total Population
40 million

Human
ORIGINS

Modern humans, *Homo sapiens*, first appeared in Africa about 200,000 years ago. However, it was another 130,000–140,000 years before they started to move out of Africa. By about 50,000 years ago, they had reached Southeast Asia and Australia.

MIGRATION OF MODERN HUMANS

Driven by the need for food and a place to settle, humans started to migrate out of Africa to other parts of the world.

'Cradle of humanity'
This region around the East African Rift Valley is where the earliest human remains have been found. From this point, modern humans set out to colonise the planet.

25k

40k

60k

50k

160k

KEY

Human finds
195k (195,000,000 years old)

65k **Human migration**
(65,000 years ago)

→ **Route of migration**

⇢ **Other possible routes**

195k

65k

155k

Into Australia
During the ice age, about 50,000 years ago, large amounts of water were frozen as ice sheets. Sea levels dropped so much that a land bridge formed, allowing humans to walk from Southeast Asia to Australia.

TIMELINE

80,000 years ago

Modern humans spread across S.E. Asia

Emergence of modern humans in Africa

Ice age begins

Modern humans begin to leave Africa

Population explosion in Africa

200,000 years ago

78,000 years ago

65,000 years ago

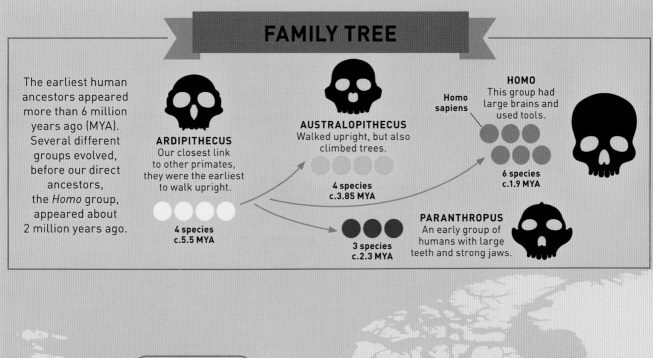

FAMILY TREE

The earliest human ancestors appeared more than 6 million years ago (MYA). Several different groups evolved, before our direct ancestors, the *Homo* group, appeared about 2 million years ago.

ARDIPITHECUS
Our closest link to other primates, they were the earliest to walk upright.

4 species
c.5.5 MYA

AUSTRALOPITHECUS
Walked upright, but also climbed trees.

4 species
c.3.85 MYA

HOMO
This group had large brains and used tools.

Homo sapiens

6 species
c.1.9 MYA

PARANTHROPUS
An early group of humans with large teeth and strong jaws.

3 species
c.2.3 MYA

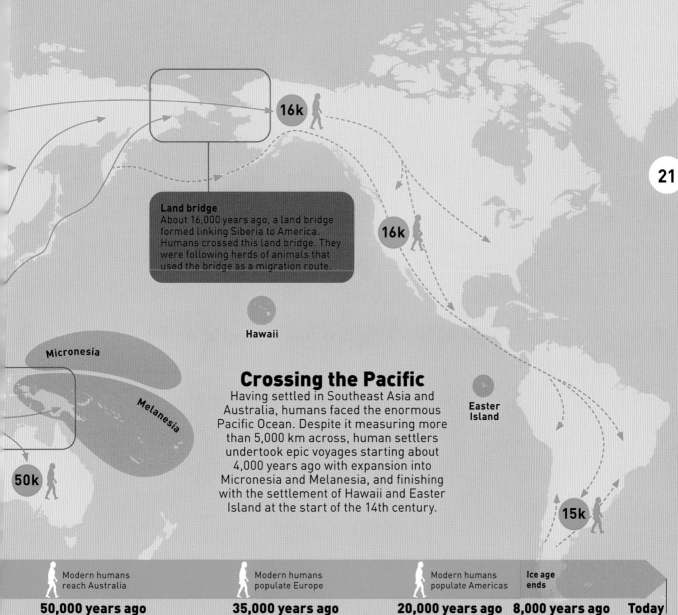

16k

16k

Land bridge
About 16,000 years ago, a land bridge formed linking Siberia to America. Humans crossed this land bridge. They were following herds of animals that used the bridge as a migration route.

Hawaii

Micronesia

Melanesia

50k

Crossing the Pacific
Having settled in Southeast Asia and Australia, humans faced the enormous Pacific Ocean. Despite it measuring more than 5,000 km across, human settlers undertook epic voyages starting about 4,000 years ago with expansion into Micronesia and Melanesia, and finishing with the settlement of Hawaii and Easter Island at the start of the 14th century.

Easter Island

15k

21

Modern humans reach Australia
50,000 years ago

Modern humans populate Europe
35,000 years ago

Modern humans populate Americas
20,000 years ago

Ice age ends
8,000 years ago

Today

Great
CIVILISATIONS

Since the first cities were founded more than 10,000 years ago, people have extended the areas they control to create kingdoms and empires. These ruled millions of people and built huge monuments to show their power.

GREAT EMPIRES

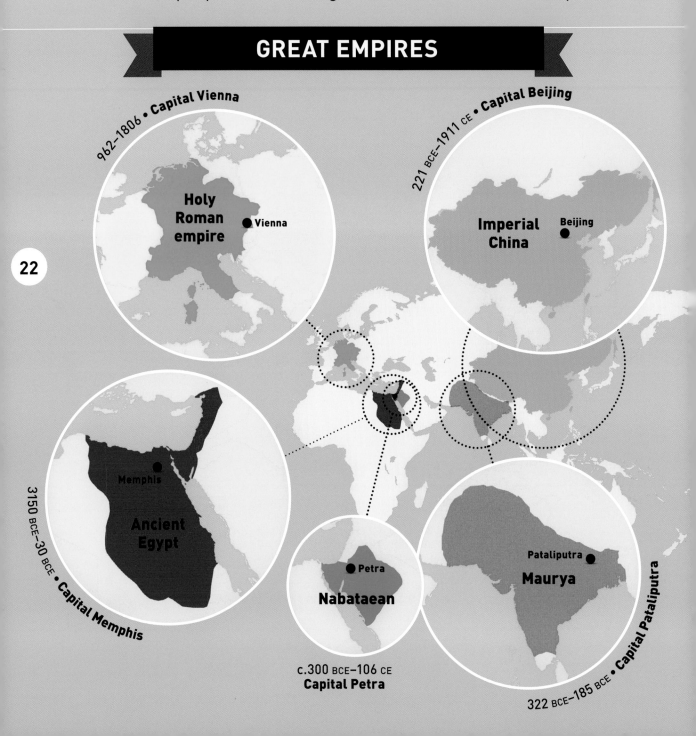

962–1806 • Capital Vienna

Holy Roman empire

● Vienna

221 BCE–1911 CE • Capital Beijing

Imperial China

● Beijing

3150 BCE–30 BCE • Capital Memphis

● Memphis

Ancient Egypt

● Petra

Nabataean

Pataliputra ●

Maurya

c.300 BCE–106 CE
Capital Petra

322 BCE–185 BCE • Capital Pataliputra

LARGEST EMPIRES

The largest empires covered millions of square kilometres. Although the British Empire was the biggest, it was scattered over several continents, making the Mongol Empire the largest continuous empire the world has ever seen.

Spanish Empire
(1492–1898)
19.4 million sq km

Russian Empire
(1723–1917)
22.8 million sq km

British Empire
(1597–1997)
33.7 million sq km

Mongol Empire
(1206–1368)
33.0 million sq km

Umayyad Caliphate
(661–751 CE)
15.0 million sq km

IMPERIAL MONUMENTS

More than 130 pyramids have been discovered in Egypt. The largest is the Pyramid of Khufu, built in 2580 BCE. It weighs as much as 16 Empire State Buildings.

c.2000 BCE–1697 CE
Capital Chichen Itza

Chichen Itza
Maya

c.1100–1533 • Capital Cuzco

Cuzco
Inca

Tenochtitlán
Aztec

c.1300–1521
Capital Tenochtitlán

Other great monuments

Teotihuacán
(100 CE) Mexico

Ziggurat of Ur (2000 BCE)
Iraq

Pyramids of Meroe
(700 BCE) Sudan

Chichen Itza
(c.1000 CE) Tikal

Types of
GOVERNMENT

People living in different countries have more or less say in how they are governed. In democracies, people can vote for their leaders, while in absolute monarchies or one-party states, people cannot choose who governs them.

THE WORLD'S GOVERNMENTS

This map shows the different types of government used by countries around the world.

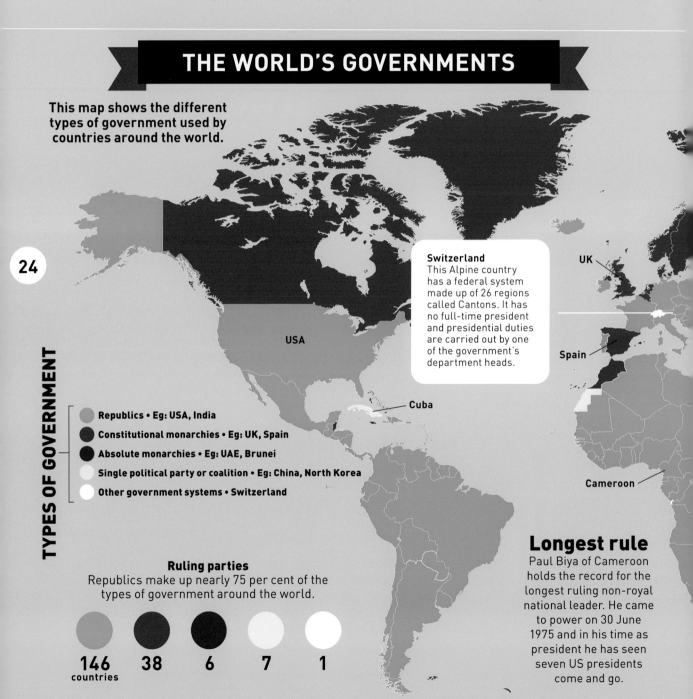

Switzerland
This Alpine country has a federal system made up of 26 regions called Cantons. It has no full-time president and presidential duties are carried out by one of the government's department heads.

UK

Spain

Cuba

Cameroon

USA

TYPES OF GOVERNMENT

- Republics • Eg: USA, India
- Constitutional monarchies • Eg: UK, Spain
- Absolute monarchies • Eg: UAE, Brunei
- Single political party or coalition • Eg: China, North Korea
- Other government systems • Switzerland

Ruling parties
Republics make up nearly 75 per cent of the types of government around the world.

146 countries	38	6	7	1

Longest rule
Paul Biya of Cameroon holds the record for the longest ruling non-royal national leader. He came to power on 30 June 1975 and in his time as president he has seen seven US presidents come and go.

53 **29**

1900 — 2015

Number of monarchs worldwide

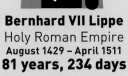

Longest-reigning monarchs

①

Sobhuza II
Swaziland
December 1899 – August 1982
82 years, 254 days

②

Bernhard VII Lippe
Holy Roman Empire
August 1429 – April 1511
81 years, 234 days

③

William IV Henneberg-Schleusingen
Holy Roman Empire
May 1480 – January 1559
78 years, 243 days

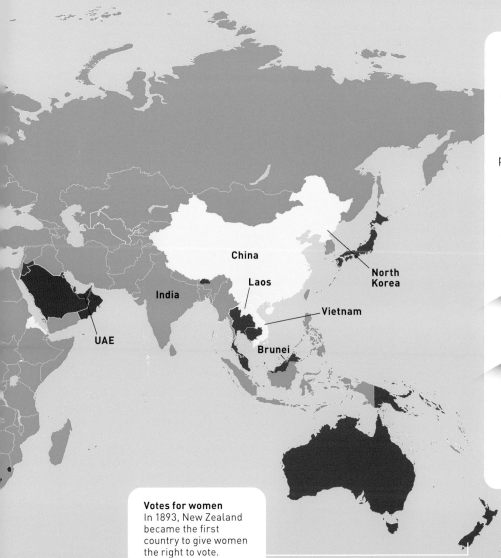

China

Laos

India

North Korea

Vietnam

UAE

Brunei

Votes for women
In 1893, New Zealand became the first country to give women the right to vote.

Communist countries

There are five nations around the world that consider themselves Communist and are governed by a single political party. They are China, Cuba, Laos, North Korea and Vietnam. These countries have a strong, central government, which owns much of the nation's industry.

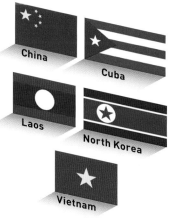

China

Cuba

Laos

North Korea

Vietnam

ARCHITECTURE

Civilisations around the world have built incredible buildings to act as places of worship, to provide protection or to display their power. Today, architects train for years to design towering skyscrapers and vast shopping centres.

HISTORIC BUILDINGS AROUND THE WORLD

This map shows the locations of some of the most famous buildings and monuments around the world.

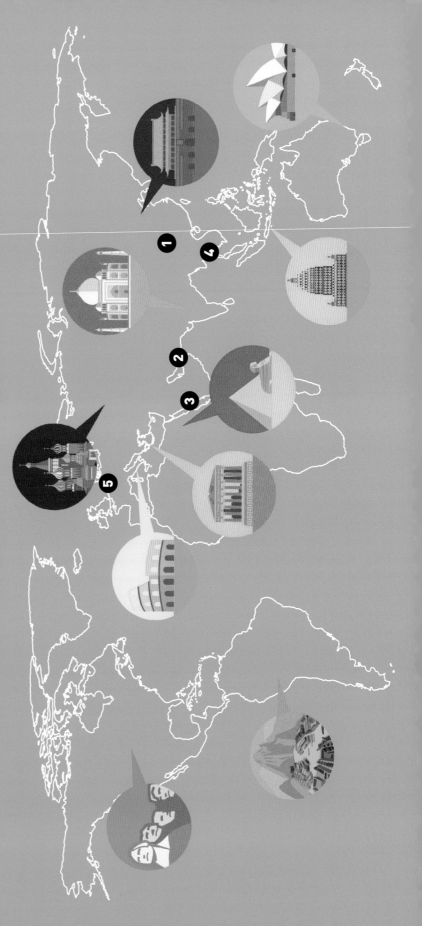

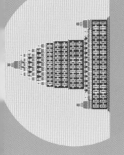

Parthenon

ATHENS, GREECE

Completed in 432 BCE, the Parthenon is a temple to Athena, the goddess after whom Athens is named. It looks down on the city from the Acropolis Hill.

St Basil's Cathedral

MOSCOW, RUSSIA

Located on Moscow's Red Square, close to the Kremlin, the brightly coloured cathedral was completed in 1561 and is now a museum.

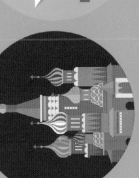

Opera House

SYDNEY, AUSTRALIA

Sydney's performing arts centre sits by the harbour and was opened in 1973. It immediately became the most famous building in Australia.

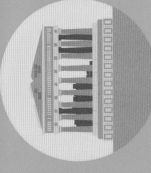

Prambanan

CENTRAL JAVA, INDONESIA

Prambanan was built in about 850 CE and is the largest Hindu temple complex in Indonesia. It has intricately carved stonework and spires rising to 47 metres.

Taj Mahal

AGRA, INDIA

Shah Jahan ruled over much of India in the mid 17th century. The Taj Mahal, completed in 1654, is a tomb for his third and favourite wife, Mumtaz Mahal.

Forbidden City

BEIJING, CHINA

Completed in 1420 by the Yongle Emperor, the Forbidden City is the world's largest palace complex, with 9,000 rooms covering an area the size of 20 football pitches.

Colosseum

ROME, ITALY

Built in 80 CE, the Colosseum was the largest amphitheatre in the Roman empire. It could hold more than 50,000 spectators and had huge sails to protect them from the sun's glare.

Mount Rushmore

SOUTH DAKOTA, USA

This huge sculpture, completed in 1939, is carved into the side of a mountain. It features the heads of four US presidents. The heads are about 18 metres tall.

Machu Picchu

CUSCO REGION, PERU

Built around 1450, the city was abandoned soon after the arrival of the Spanish in South America. It remained hidden to the outside world until 1911.

Pyramids

GIZA, EGYPT

Built in about 2500 BCE, the three Great Pyramids at Giza are part of a large burial complex. A colossal sculpture called the Great Sphinx sits in front of them.

— LARGEST BUILDINGS BY FLOOR AREA —

❶ *New Century Global Center* (Chengdu, China) 1,760,000 sq m
❷ *Dubai International Airport Terminal 3* (Dubai, UAE) 1,713,000 sq m
❸ *Abraj Al-Bait Endowment* (Mecca, Saudi Arabia) 1,575,815 sq m
❹ *CentralWorld* (Bangkok, Thailand) 1,024,000 sq m
❺ *Aalsmeer Flower Auction* (Aalsmeer, Netherlands) 990,000 sq m

NEW CENTURY GLOBAL CENTER, CHENGDU

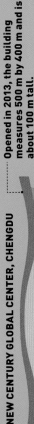
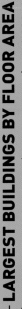

Opened in 2013, the building measures 500 m by 400 m and is about 100 m tall.

It's big enough to fit the Sydney Opera House inside 20 times.

Tallest
BUILDINGS

With space in many cities being limited, architects and planners choose to build up rather than spread out, creating ever taller skyscrapers with dozens of floors. Today's giants are nearly a kilometre tall and contain more than 100 storeys.

TALLEST BUILDINGS ON EACH CONTINENT

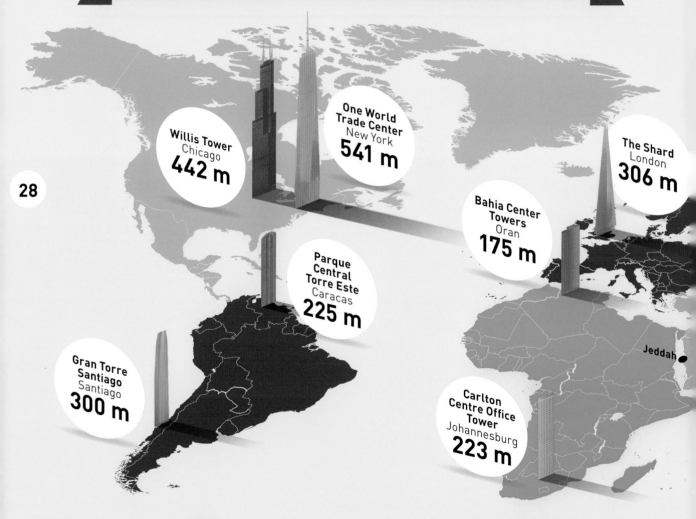

Willis Tower
Chicago
442 m

One World Trade Center
New York
541 m

The Shard
London
306 m

Bahia Center Towers
Oran
175 m

Parque Central Torre Este
Caracas
225 m

Gran Torre Santiago
Santiago
300 m

Carlton Centre Office Tower
Johannesburg
223 m

Jeddah

KEY

- NORTH AMERICA
- EUROPE
- ASIA
- SOUTH AMERICA
- AFRICA
- OCEANIA

Key regions for skyscraper building include the Middle East, where oil-rich countries are investing their wealth in huge building plans, and Russia, whose capital city, Moscow, has seven of Europe's ten tallest buildings. They were all built in the last 10 years.

Kingdom Tower

Currently under construction, the Kingdom Tower in Jeddah will be 1,000 m tall when it is completed in 2019 (the Burj Khalifa is only 830 m tall). It will have 167 floors above ground (4 below), 57 elevators and have 530 apartments, 200 hotel rooms and parking for 3,190 vehicles.

Most skyscrapers

China has more skyscrapers (taller than 150 m) than any other country.

China **1,284**
USA **694**
Japan **200**
UAE **195**
South Korea **192**

Kingdom Tower

Burj Khalifa

Tallest cities in the world

The cities listed here have more skyscrapers than any other. The numbers show how many buildings in each city have a height greater than 150 metres.

Hong Kong **315**

New York **241**

Dubai **152**

Shanghai **130**
Tokyo **114**
Chicago **113**
Guangzhou **92**
Chongqing **83**
Shenzhen **82**

Mercury City
Moscow
339 m

Burj Khalifa
Dubai
828 m

Shanghai Tower
Shanghai
632 m

Shenzhen
Chongqing

Guangzhou

Hong Kong

Tokyo

Q1 Tower
Gold Coast City
322 m

Eureka Tower
Melbourne
297 m

29

Population GROWTH

How quickly a population grows depends on a number of things, including the standard of healthcare, how many children are born, how long people live for and how rich they are. While the populations of some countries and regions are growing very quickly, others are predicted to get smaller!

MOST POPULATED COUNTRIES

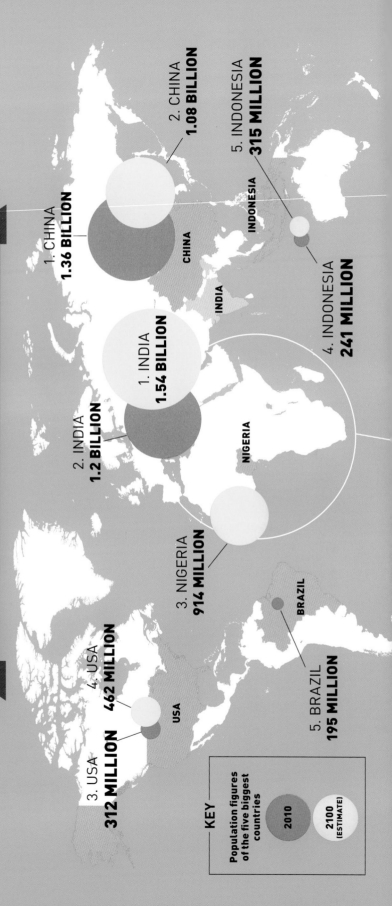

1. CHINA
1.36 BILLION

2. CHINA
1.08 BILLION

5. INDONESIA
315 MILLION

CHINA

INDONESIA

INDIA

INDONESIA

2. INDIA
1.2 BILLION

1. INDIA
1.54 BILLION

4. INDONESIA
241 MILLION

NIGERIA

3. NIGERIA
914 MILLION

3. USA
312 MILLION

4. USA
462 MILLION

USA

BRAZIL

5. BRAZIL
195 MILLION

KEY

Population figures of the five biggest countries

2010

2100 (ESTIMATE)

Fertility rates

The average number of children each woman gives birth to in her lifetime is known as the fertility rate. If the fertility rate is high, then it is likely that a country's population is growing quickly. These figures show some of the highest and lowest fertility rates in the world.

Countries with some of the highest fertility rates (children per woman).

NIGER 6.89

AFGHANISTAN 5.43

Countries with some of the lowest fertility rates (children per woman).

SINGAPORE 0.80

SOUTH KOREA 1.25

TEN FASTEST-GROWING POPULATIONS

1. LEBANON 9.37%
4. JORDAN 3.86%
5. QATAR 3.58%
3. SOUTH SUDAN 4.12%
9. UGANDA 3.24%
6. MALAWI 3.33%
2. ZIMBABWE 4.36%
8. BURUNDI 3.28%
10. LIBYA 3.08%
7. NIGER 3.28%

This map shows the ten fastest-growing countries and the percentages their populations are growing by each year.

Bigger and bigger

With the fastest-growing countries located in Africa, the population of that continent will shoot up over the next 100 years. By 2100, it will have nearly quadrupled in size.

Predicted populations of each continent from 2010 to 2100:

POPULATION 2010

AFRICA 1.1 billion
ASIA 4.3 billion
EUROPE 740 million
NORTH AMERICA 556 million
SOUTH AMERICA 401 million
OCEANIA 38 million

POPULATION 2100 (ESTIMATE)

AFRICA 4.2 billion
ASIA 4.7 billion
EUROPE 639 million
NORTH AMERICA 513 million
SOUTH AMERICA 467 million
OCEANIA 47 million

Average family

Levels of wealth vary greatly around the world. In general, richer countries grow more slowly than poorer ones. People in poorer countries, such as Burkina Faso in Africa, tend to have larger families than those in richer countries, such as the USA. This increases the number of family members who can earn money and also means that older children can care for the old and very young.

Average household size USA **2.6**

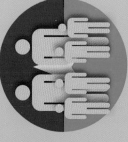

Average household size BURKINA FASO **5.9**

The Name
GAME

Around 353,000 babies are born around the world every day. That's more than four babies every second. The names of these babies vary depending on their gender, the country they are born in and their religion.

POPULAR BABY NAMES AROUND THE WORLD

This world map shows some of the most popular children's names in countries around the world, as well as the most common surnames.

Emma	Liam
Olivia	Jackson
Sophia	Logan
Zoe	Lucas
Emily	Noah

CANADA

USA

USA
Smith

Emma	Liam
Olivia	Noah
Sophia	Ethan
Ava	Mason
Mia	Lucas

Fatima	Mohamed
Khadija	Ahmed
Aicha	Mohammed
Malika	Said
Naima	Rachid

Mexico
Martínez

BRAZIL

Brazil
Silva

KEY

Popular baby names
Girls

Popular baby names
Boys

Country
Name

Most common surnames
The spread of surnames may depend upon a country's history. For example, the spread of the British Empire during the 18th and 19th centuries can be seen by the occurrence of British surnames, such as Smith, in English-speaking countries around the globe.

Sophia	Miguel
Julia	David
Alice	Arthur
Manuela	Gabriel
Isabella	Pedro

Amelia
Olivia
Isla
Emily
Poppy

Oliver
Jack
Harry
Jacob
Charlie

A woman from Hartlepool, UK, may have the record for the longest name in the world. Changing her name to raise money for charity, her full name is …

Red – Wacky League – Antlez – Broke the Stereo – Neon Tide – Bring Back Honesty – Coalition – Feedback – Hand of Aces – Keep Going Captain – Let's Pretend – Lost State of Dance – Paper Taxis – Lunar Road – Up! Down! Strange! – All and I – Neon Sheep – Eve Hornby – Faye Bradley – AJ Wilde – Michael Rice – Dion Watts – Matthew Appleyard – John Ashurst – Lauren Swales – Zoe Angus – Jaspreet Singh – Emma Matthews – Nicola Brown – Leanne Pickering – Victoria Davies – Rachel Burnside – Gil Parker – Freya Watson – Alisha Watts – James Pearson – Jacob Sotheran–Darley – Beth Lowery – Jasmine Hewitt – Chloe Gibson – Molly Farquhar – Lewis Murphy – Abbie Coulson – Nick Davies – Harvey Parker – Kyran Williamson – Michael Anderson – Bethany Murray – Sophie Hamilton – Amy Wilkins – Emma Simpson – Liam Wales – Jacob Bartram – Alex Hooks – Rebecca Miller – Caitlin Miller – Sean McCloskey – Dominic Parker – Abbey Sharpe – Elena Larkin – Rebecca Simpson – Nick Dixon – Abbie Farrelly – Liam Grieves – Casey Smith – Liam Downing – Ben Wignall – Elizabeth Hann – Danielle Walker – Lauren Glen – James Johnson – Ben Ervine – Kate Burton – James Hudson – Daniel Mayes – Matthew Kitching – Josh Bennett – Evolution – Dreams.

UK
Smith

Ireland
Murphy

France
Martin

UK

Germany
Müller

Italy
Rossi

Spain
García

ITALY

Sofia
Giulia
Aurora
Giorgia
Martina

Francesco
Alessandro
Lorenzo
Andrea
Leonardo

Sakura
Riko
Aoi
Wakana
Sara

Minato
Sou
Ichika
Itsuki
Tatsuki

Sofia
Maria
Anastasia
Anna
Yelizaveta

Alexander
Maxim
Artem
Mikhail
Ivan

Russia
Smirnov

RUSSIA

33

China
Wang

CHINA

JAPAN

Japan
Sato

INDIA

Aadya
Diya
Saanvi
Amaira
Angel

Aarav
Reyansh
Mohammad
Vivaan
Ayaan

Wang Fang
Wang Xiu Ying
Li Xiu Wing
Li Na
Zhang Xiu Wing

Zhang Wei
Wang Weo
Li Wei
Liu Wei
Li Qiang

MOROCCO

NIGERIA

KENYA

Esther
Abigail
Rose
Stephanie
Temitope

Emmanuel
Michael
Victor
Peter
Kingsley

Faith
Winnie
Linda
Sharon
Anne

John
James
Martin
David
Joseph

AUSTRALIA

Olivia
Charlotte
Mia
Ava
Amelia

Oliver
William
Jack
Noah
Jackson

Australia
Smith

Global Emissions and
POPULATION

Carbon dioxide (CO_2) is the most common greenhouse gas that is responsible for climate change. It is present naturally and it is released by human activities such as energy production and industry.

WORLD'S BIGGEST CO_2 EMITTERS

This world map shows the countries with the largest populations and those that release the most CO_2. It also shows those countries whose people produce the most CO_2 per head.

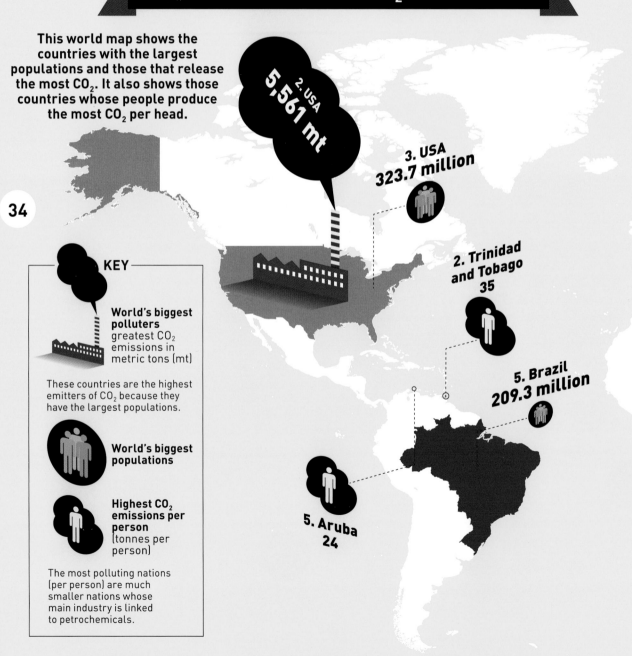

2. USA
5,561 mt

3. USA
323.7 million

2. Trinidad and Tobago
35

5. Brazil
209.3 million

5. Aruba
24

KEY

World's biggest polluters greatest CO_2 emissions in metric tons (mt)

These countries are the highest emitters of CO_2 because they have the largest populations.

World's biggest populations

Highest CO_2 emissions per person (tonnes per person)

The most polluting nations (per person) are much smaller nations whose main industry is linked to petrochemicals.

Since 1751, **about 1,480 gigatonnes** (billions of tonnes) **of carbon dioxide** have been released by industrial activity.

More than half of this **(50.2% or 743 gigatonnes)** has been released since 1988.

HISTORICAL EMISSIONS

The countries listed here have released the greatest combined amounts of carbon dioxide since 1850.

USA 361,300.0 million tonnes

China 140,860.3 million tonnes

Russia 101,116.7 million tonnes

Germany 84,123.6 million tonnes

UK 70,042.3 million tonnes

1. China
9,680 mt

4. Russia
1,595 mt

1. China
1.381 billion

5. Japan
1,232 mt

3. Kuwait
27

3. India
2,597 mt

4. Indonesia
260 million

1. Qatar
46

The world produces about 36.1 billion mt **of CO$_2$** every year.

2. India
1.324 billion

4. Brunei
Darussalam
24.0

People and
ENERGY

This image shows the world at night, revealing where the main concentrations of people live. However, the brightest areas aren't always the most populated, as richer countries will use more electricity per person, and appear brighter, than poorer ones.

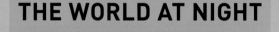

THE WORLD AT NIGHT

Toronto

36

Canada has a population of just 3.5 people per square kilometre.

CANADA
Area: 10 million square kilometres
Population: 36.2 million

Most Canadians live in a few large cities, such as Toronto, leaving vast areas with very few people that are very dark in this image.

Each person in the USA uses 12,500 kWh.

USA
Energy consumption:
4 trillion kilowatt hours (kWh)
Population: 323.7 million

The USA has a population of about 320 million. However, the people in this rich country use so much energy that they are the second largest users of electricity in the world.

THE WORLD'S POPULATION USES MORE THAN **20 TRILLION KWH** OF ELECTRICITY A YEAR.

The USA accounts for about 20 per cent of this.

BIGGEST ENERGY CONSUMERS
(BILLION KWH)

China
4,831

USA
3,883

Russia
1,037

Japan
859.7

India
757.9

BIGGEST POPULATIONS

USA
323.7 million

Indonesia
260 million

Brazil
209.2 million

China
1.357 billion

India
1.324 billion

EGYPT/THE NILE

Nearly all of Egypt's population of about 87 million people live in a thin band on either side of the Nile.

Two Koreas

The Korean peninsula is split into two nations: North Korea and South Korea. The tiny dot of light in the northern half shows the location of North Korea's capital city – Pyongyang.

NORTH KOREA

Energy consumption: 18 billion kWh

Population: 25 million

37

Pyongyang

SOUTH KOREA

Energy consumption: 450 billion kWh

Population: 50 million

NIGERIA

Energy consumption:
20.4 billion kWh

Population: 182 million

The population of Nigeria is more than half that of the USA. However, each person only uses 115 kWh – less than one tenth of the amount used by a citizen of the USA. This is why the country appears so dark.

Each person in Nigeria uses 115 kWh.

(•) **Brisbane**

Perth (•)

(•) **Sydney**

(•) **Melbourne**

AUSTRALIA

Area: 7.7 million square kilometres

Population: 24.2 million

Nearly 55 per cent of Australia's population of 24.2 million live in its four largest cities – Sydney, Melbourne, Brisbane and Perth – which lie dotted along the country's east and western coasts.

OIL

Every day, 89.08 million of barrels of oil are pumped out of the ground and carried along pipelines and in enormous tankers to refineries. Here, the oil is processed to produce petroleum and other products, including gas and plastics.

BIGGEST OIL PRODUCERS

This map shows the world's biggest producers of oil. These countries pump oil out of the ground using land-based wells or huge sea-based oil rigs.

Canada
4.4
million barrels per day

What oil is used for?

Crude oil is transported to large oil refineries, where it is treated and turned into a wide range of products. The image below shows some of the major products created by refining oil. In the USA, petrol accounts for 46 per cent of refined oil products, while heating oil and diesel account for 20 per cent.

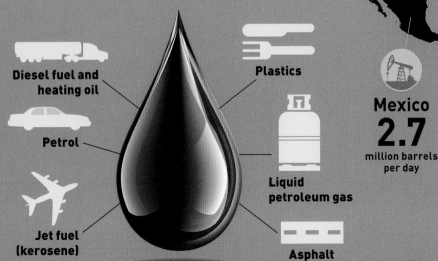

Diesel fuel and heating oil

Petrol

Jet fuel (kerosene)

Plastics

Liquid petroleum gas

Asphalt

USA
13.7
million barrels per day

Mexico
2.7
million barrels per day

BIGGEST IMPORTERS

Some countries have such high energy demands that they need to import oil as well as producing it. The USA, for example, is one of the world's biggest oil producers, but it's also the world's biggest importer of oil.

Top world oil net importers (thousand barrels per day)

= 1,000 barrels

Germany 1,830

China 6,167

Japan 3,441

Philippines 1,503

USA 9,080

India 3,812

South Korea 2,949

Italy 1,346

Russia
11
million barrels per day

39

Iraq
4

Kuwait
2.7

Strait of Hormuz

Iran
3.4
million barrels per day

UAE
3.5
million barrels per day

China
4.6
million barrels per day

Strait of Malacca

Saudi Arabia
11.9
million barrels per day

Busiest shipping routes

There are a number of points where sea routes are narrow, creating busy shipping lanes. The world's busiest shipping routes for oil are the Strait of Hormuz (17 million barrels per day) and the Strait of Malacca (15.2 million barrels per day).

FORESTS

The world's forests are not evenly distributed around the globe – two-thirds of them lie in just ten countries: Russia, Brazil, Canada, USA, China, Australia, Congo, Indonesia, Peru and India. However, these forests are under threat as trees are cut down for fuel or to make way for farms and towns.

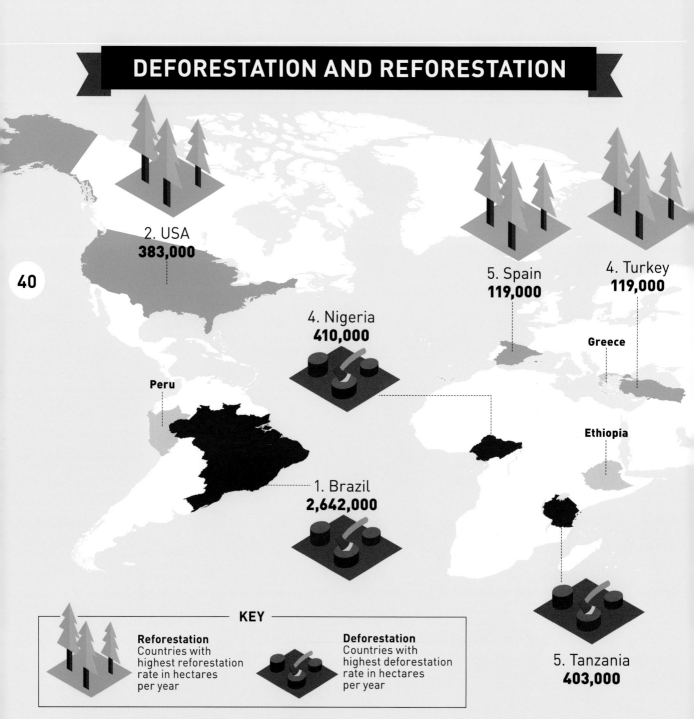

DEFORESTATION AND REFORESTATION

2. USA
383,000

5. Spain
119,000

4. Turkey
119,000

4. Nigeria
410,000

Greece

Peru

Ethiopia

1. Brazil
2,642,000

5. Tanzania
403,000

KEY

Reforestation
Countries with highest reforestation rate in hectares per year

Deforestation
Countries with highest deforestation rate in hectares per year

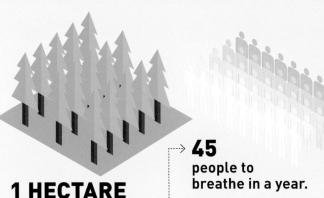

1 HECTARE
of trees will produce
enough oxygen for

45
people to
breathe in a year.

Reforestation

The Bonn Challenge sees countries committing to restoring 150 million hectares of forest by 2020 – that's a bigger area than the whole of Peru.

20%

The biggest commitment to reforestation is by **Ethiopia**, which has pledged to restore **22 million hectares** (more than 20 per cent of its land area).

THE AMAZONIAN RAINFOREST ALONE PRODUCES ABOUT **20 PER CENT** OF THE WORLD'S OXYGEN.

Global deforestation rate

In total, nearly
13 million hectares
of forest are lost each year.
This is an area equivalent
to Greece.

41

1. China
2,986,000

3. Vietnam
207,000

3. Indonesia
498,000

2. Australia

Rare species

One of the rarest species in the world is the Wollemi pine. It was thought to be extinct until about 100 trees were discovered in a remote valley near Sydney, Australia, 1994. The species is at least 200 million years old.

PALM OIL

The fruit of the oil palm produces an oil that is used in a wide range of products – in fact, it can be found in nearly half of everything you buy. Today, nearly 60 million tonnes of palm oil are produced each year and the surge in demand for this substance in the last 50 years has led to a dramatic increase in deforestation rates in countries growing the crop.

PALM OIL PRODUCTION

This map shows the increase in annual production rates in millions of tonnes by the world's major palm oil producers between 1964 and 2015.

THAILAND
2015 **2.25**
1964 **0**

DEMOCRATIC REPUBLIC OF THE CONGO
2015 **0.21**
1964 **0.13**

NIGERIA
2015 **0.93**
1964 **0.54**

COLOMBIA
2015 **1.11**
1964 **0**

HONDURAS
2015 **0.44**
1964 **0**

ECUADOR
2015 **0.57**
1964 **0**

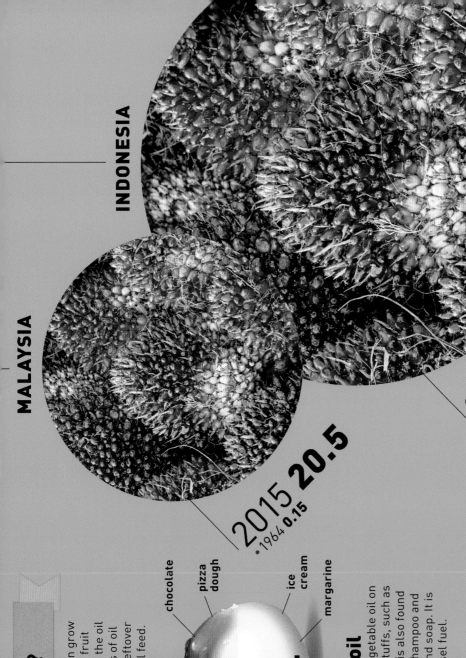

MALAYSIA

INDONESIA

2015 **20.5**
• 1964 **0.15**

2015 **33**
• 1964 **0.16**

WHAT IS IT?

The oil palm is a tree that can grow 20 metres tall. It produces fruit that is processed to produce the oil at a rate of about 4.5 tonnes of oil per hectare each year. The leftover fibre is used to make animal feed.

chocolate

pizza dough

ice cream

margarine

Each piece of fruit contains
50% OIL

biodiesel

detergent

shampoo

soap

lipstick

uses for palm oil

Palm oil is the most widely used vegetable oil on the planet. It is used to make foodstuffs, such as pizza, ice cream and chocolate. It is also found in cleaning materials, including shampoo and detergent, as well as cosmetics and soap. It is even used to produce biodiesel fuel.

deforestation

Every year, millions of hectares of forest are cleared to make room for palm oil plantations. Between 2000 and 2012, Thailand lost about 6 million hectares of forest, which is about half the size of England, for plantations. As the forest disappears, so animal species, such as the orang-utan, face threats to their existence.

IN THE TIME IT WILL TAKE YOU TO READ THIS PAGE **2 FOOTBALL PITCHES OF RAINFOREST** WILL HAVE BEEN CLEARED TO MAKE WAY FOR PALM OIL PLANTATIONS.

CLIMATE

Types of climate vary greatly around the world, depending largely on a region's location between the Equator and the poles. They can be hot or cold, have huge differences in the amount of rain they get, and they can have different seasons, where conditions vary from one month to the next.

WORLD CLIMATE TYPES

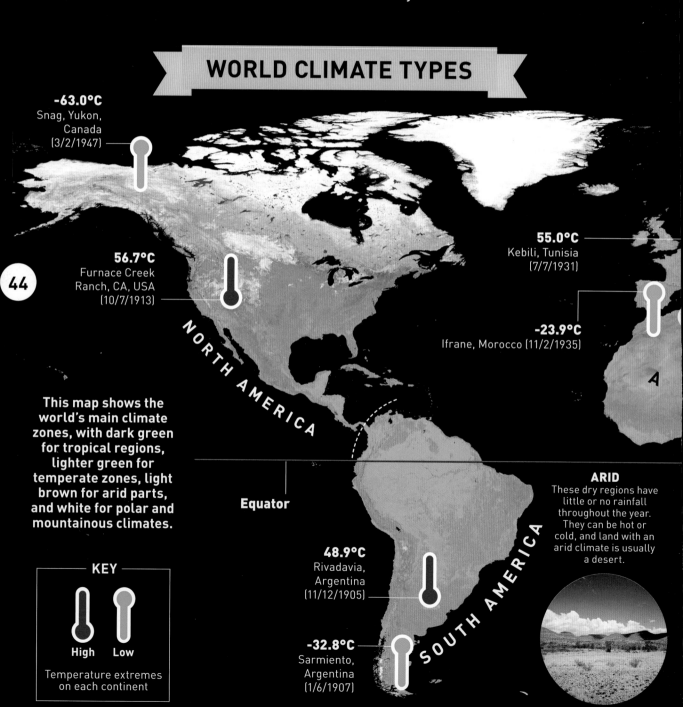

-63.0°C
Snag, Yukon, Canada
(3/2/1947)

56.7°C
Furnace Creek Ranch, CA, USA
(10/7/1913)

55.0°C
Kebili, Tunisia
(7/7/1931)

-23.9°C
Ifrane, Morocco (11/2/1935)

44

NORTH AMERICA

SOUTH AMERICA

This map shows the world's main climate zones, with dark green for tropical regions, lighter green for temperate zones, light brown for arid parts, and white for polar and mountainous climates.

Equator

48.9°C
Rivadavia, Argentina
(11/12/1905)

-32.8°C
Sarmiento, Argentina
(1/6/1907)

A

ARID
These dry regions have little or no rainfall throughout the year. They can be hot or cold, and land with an arid climate is usually a desert.

KEY

High   Low

Temperature extremes on each continent

MEDITERRANEAN

Named after the climate around the Mediterranean Sea, this climate is found in other parts of the world, such as Chile, California, USA, and South Africa. It has warm, dry summers and cool, wet winters.

TEMPERATE

Temperate zones lie midway between the tropics and the poles. They usually have mild summers and winters and rainfall levels can be high throughout the year.

POLAR

The climates around the poles are cold throughout the year, but especially during the winter months when the Sun may not rise above the horizon. Close to the poles, sea and ground are covered by thick sheets of ice.

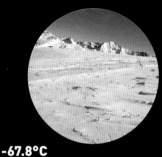

48.0°C
Athens, Greece
(10/7/1977)

-58.1°C
Ust 'Schugor, Russia
(21/12/1978)

-67.8°C
Verkoyansk and Oimekon, Russia
(5/2/1892, 7/2/1892, 6/2/1933)

EUROPE

ASIA

45

54.0°C
Tirat Tsvi, Israel
(21/6/1942)

RICA

MOUNTAINS

Highland regions, such as the Andes and the Himalayas, have no distinct seasons. Conditions vary the higher you climb.

OCEANIA

TROPICAL

Tropical regions lie on either side of the Equator. They can be tropical wet, with high levels of rainfall throughout the year, or tropical dry, with two distinct seasons – a wet season and a dry one.

50.7°C
Oodnadatta,
Australia
(2/1/1960)

-23.0°C
Charlotte Pass, NSW,
Australia (29/6/1994)

Climate
CHANGE

Throughout its history, Earth's temperatures have varied, creating ice ages and warmer periods. Scientists believe that temperatures could increase by as much as 6°C over the next century, and this could have dramatic effects.

RISING SEA LEVELS

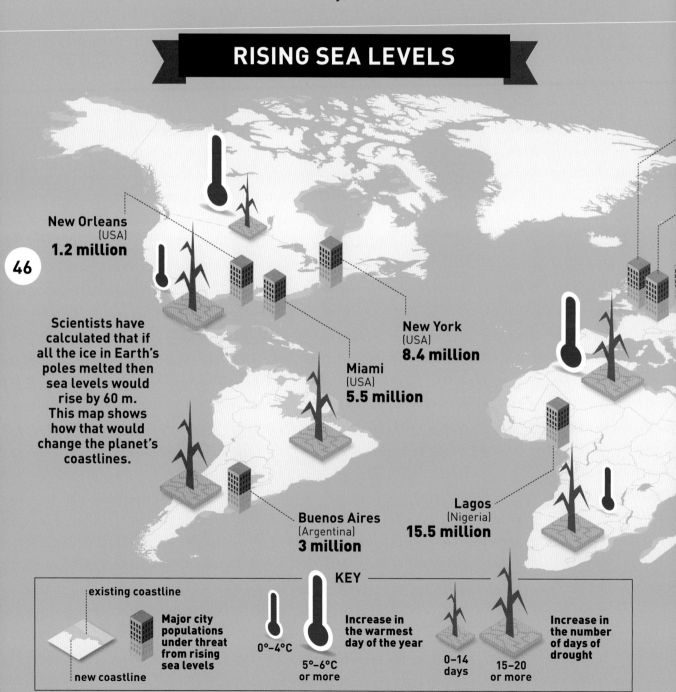

New Orleans
(USA)
1.2 million

Scientists have calculated that if all the ice in Earth's poles melted then sea levels would rise by 60 m. This map shows how that would change the planet's coastlines.

New York
(USA)
8.4 million

Miami
(USA)
5.5 million

Buenos Aires
(Argentina)
3 million

Lagos
(Nigeria)
15.5 million

KEY

existing coastline

new coastline

Major city populations under threat from rising sea levels

0°–4°C

5°–6°C or more

Increase in the warmest day of the year

0–14 days

15–20 or more

Increase in the number of days of drought

COSTS TO MAJOR CITIES IF SEA LEVELS RISE

Miami (USA) US$3.5 trillion
Guangzhou (China) US$3.4 trillion
New York (USA) US$2.1 trillion
Kolkata (India) US$2 trillion
Shanghai (China) US$1.8 trillion

London (UK)
8.6 million

Amsterdam (Netherlands)
1.6 million

Copenhagen (Denmark)
1.9 million

Kolkata (India)
11.8 million

Dhaka
(Bangladesh)
17.5 million

Drought

A drought is when a region experiences below-average rainfall for an extended period of time. Droughts can cause crops to fail, leading to famine. The worst famine in history occurred in 1876–1879 in northern China when there was little rainfall for three years, leading to between 9–13 million deaths.

Shanghai
(China)
23.9 million

Mumbai
(India)
21 million

Tokyo
(Japan)
37.8 million

Guangzhou
(China)
10.3 million

Hong Kong
(China)
7.2 million

Ho Chi Minh City
(Vietnam)
9.2 million

BIODIVERSITY

Some parts of the world, such as rainforests, are home to thousands of different types, or species, of living things, while others, such as the poles and hot deserts, may only have a handful.

BIODIVERSITY RANGE AND HOTSPOTS

This map shows the countries with the highest and lowest numbers of species. This variation of species is known as the region's biodiversity.

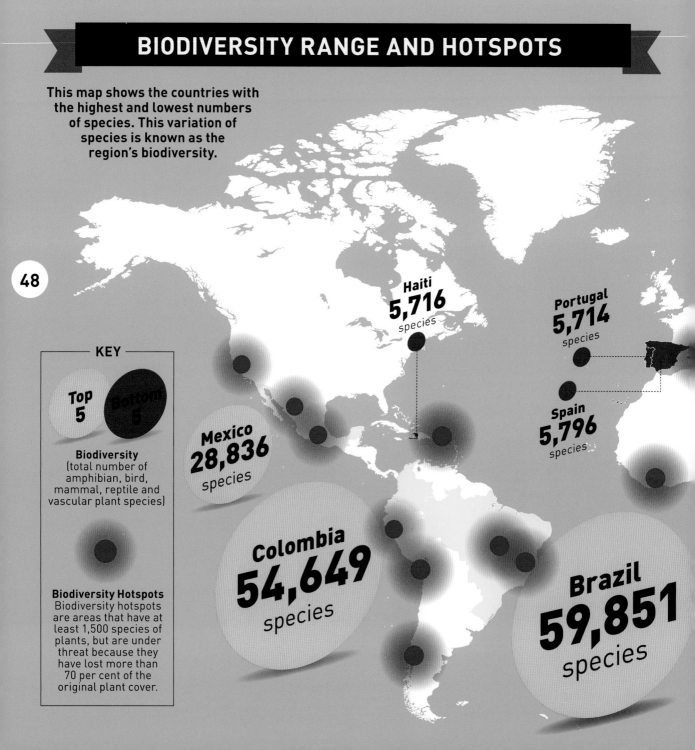

48

KEY

Top 5

Bottom 5

Biodiversity
(total number of amphibian, bird, mammal, reptile and vascular plant species)

Biodiversity Hotspots
Biodiversity hotspots are areas that have at least 1,500 species of plants, but are under threat because they have lost more than 70 per cent of the original plant cover.

Haiti
5,716
species

Portugal
5,714
species

Spain
5,796
species

Mexico
28,836
species

Colombia
54,649
species

Brazil
59,851
species

NUMBER OF SPECIES IN THE WORLD

Thousands of new species are discovered every year, and estimates show that there are far more species that are yet to be found.

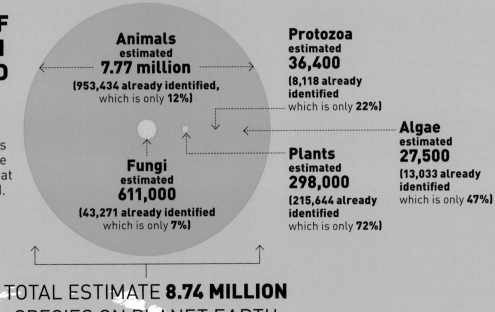

Animals
estimated
7.77 million
(953,434 already identified, which is only **12%**)

Protozoa
estimated
36,400
(8,118 already identified which is only **22%**)

Fungi
estimated
611,000
(43,271 already identified which is only **7%**)

Plants
estimated
298,000
(215,644 already identified which is only **72%**)

Algae
estimated
27,500
(13,033 already identified which is only **47%**)

TOTAL ESTIMATE **8.74 MILLION** SPECIES ON PLANET EARTH

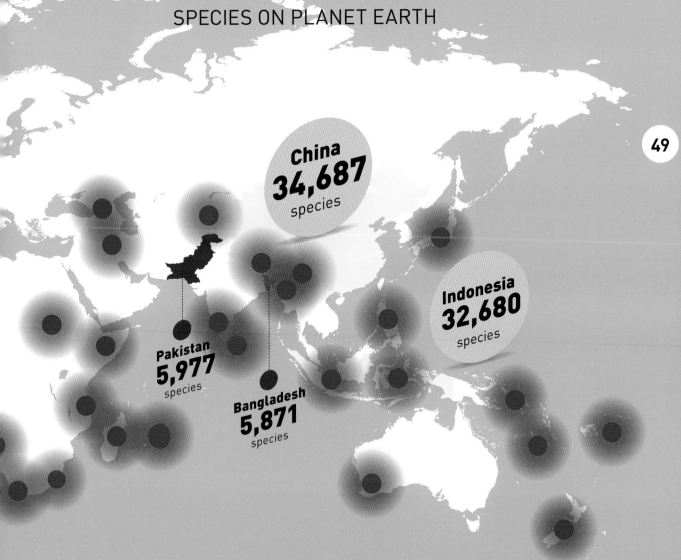

China
34,687
species

Indonesia
32,680
species

Pakistan
5,977
species

Bangladesh
5,871
species

Endangered
SPECIES

Scientists believe that more than 20,000 species of plants and animals are on the brink of extinction. This includes about one-third of all amphibian species, a quarter of the world's mammals and an eighth of all bird species.

THREATENED SPECIES

This world map shows how many species of plant and animal are under threat in a selection of countries from around the planet.

CANADA

USA
1,203

UK

MEXICO
959

FRANCE

NIGER

CENTRAL AFRICAN REP.

SENEGAL

Under threat

In general, those countries that have a great range of biodiversity, such as those that contain rainforests, have the highest number of species under threat. The country with the highest number of threatened species is Ecuador.

48
are molluscs

26
are reptiles

43
are mammals

93
are birds

Ecuador has
2,282
ENDANGERED
SPECIES,
of which...

171
are amphibians

1,837
are plants

14
are invertebrates

50
are fish

CAMEROON
632

BRAZIL
1,008

ARGENTINA

Why do species become endangered?

There are many reasons why plant and animal species become endangered. Some species are worth a lot of money and are collected or hunted, while other species are threatened by pollution and disease. Perhaps the greatest threats come from habitat loss, climate change and the appearance of foreign species.

Habitat loss
Habitat destruction, such as the clearing of forests for mines or cities, reduces the area a species can live in, as well as its food supply.

Climate change
A change in a region's climate can destroy a habitat and reduce the amount of food sources, making it difficult for a species to survive.

Invasive species
A new, foreign species may compete for the same food as a native species, or it can even feed on the native species, reducing its numbers.

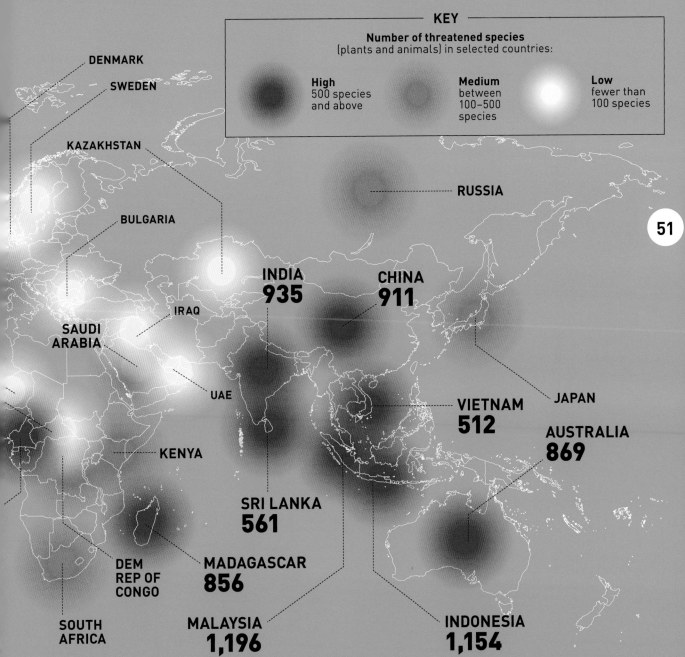

KEY

Number of threatened species (plants and animals) in selected countries:

High
500 species and above

Medium
between 100–500 species

Low
fewer than 100 species

DENMARK

SWEDEN

KAZAKHSTAN

RUSSIA

BULGARIA

INDIA
935

CHINA
911

IRAQ

SAUDI ARABIA

UAE

VIETNAM
512

JAPAN

AUSTRALIA
869

KENYA

SRI LANKA
561

DEM REP OF CONGO

MADAGASCAR
856

SOUTH AFRICA

MALAYSIA
1,196

INDONESIA
1,154

Adapting for SURVIVAL

Around the world, different animals have evolved different characteristics to suit their environment and way of life. This can include thick fur to stay warm in the polar chill or a super-long neck to grasp food that's far out of the reach of others.

ANIMAL HABITATS

Polar bears

RANGE
ARCTIC

Polar bears have thick fur and a layer of fat to keep them warm in the freezing Arctic. They can also swim for many kilometres from one patch of sea ice to another in search of prey.

Saltwater crocodiles

RANGE
EASTERN INDIA, SOUTHEAST ASIA AND NORTHERN AUSTRALIA

These huge reptiles use their enormous size to ambush and overpower prey. They have powerful tails to push them through the water and their eyes and noses are on top of their heads so that they can remain submerged and out of sight of their unsuspecting prey.

Kangaroos

RANGE
AUSTRALIA

Kangaroos have long, powerful legs, which they use to bound across the large grasslands of Australia.

Gorillas

RANGE
AFRICA

Gorillas have thick fur to protect their skin from biting insects and to keep them warm. They have large teeth to help them chew the plants and leaves that make up their diet.

Camels

RANGE
AFRICA, MIDDLE EAST AND SOUTH ASIA

Camels have adapted to life in dry desert climates. They have long eyelashes to keep sand out of their eyes and they can close their nostrils to keep sand out of their noses. Their humps are full of fat and act as a food store, and they have huge feet so that they don't sink into the sand.

Giraffes

RANGE
AFRICA

Giraffes use their long necks to reach leaves high up in trees and out of reach of other animals' grasp. They are also able to spot far-away predators. They have strong hearts to push blood up to their heads.

53

Wandering albatross

RANGE
SOUTHERN OCEAN

Albatrosses have long, thin wings, which they use to catch ocean winds and glide for hours on end without even a single flap.

Blue whale

RANGE
ALL OCEANS

The largest animal that has ever lived is able to grow to enormous size because its body weight is supported by water. Its mouth is filled with large frills called baleen plates, which the whale uses to filter out tiny creatures, called plankton, from the water to eat.

African elephant

RANGE
AFRICA

The largest land animal on the planet has huge ears, which it uses to control its body heat. Its long trunk is used to pick up food and objects, scoop up water, sniff things and to feel and communicate with other elephants.

Octopus

RANGE
ALL OCEANS

This mollusc doesn't have an internal skeleton. This means that it can squeeze its body into tiny cracks to hide from predators or to search for prey.

Animal
MIGRATION

Many animals take part in regular journeys in search of food, water or to find somewhere to give birth and raise young. These migrations can cover thousands of kilometres or just a few hundred metres.

MAJOR MIGRATION ROUTES

This map shows some of the greatest migrations undertaken by different animals over land and sea, and through the air.

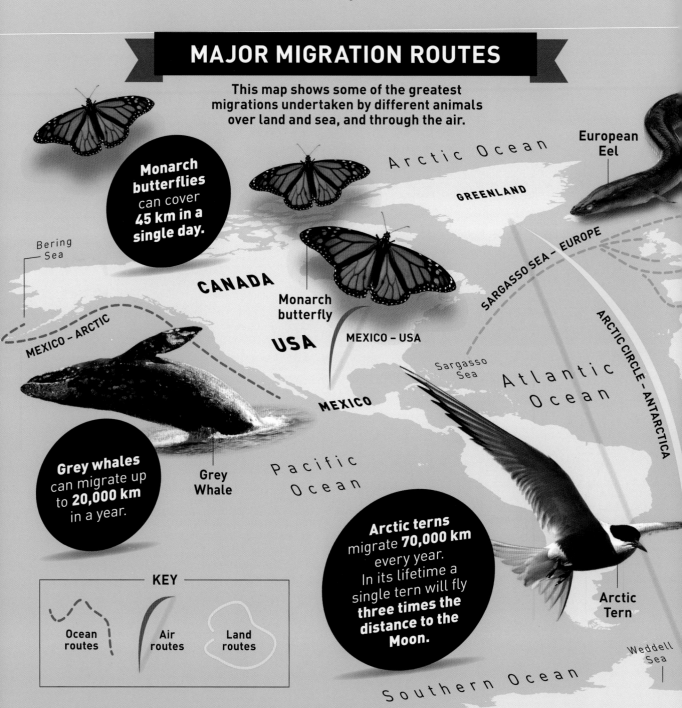

European Eel

Arctic Ocean

GREENLAND

Monarch butterflies can cover **45 km in a single day.**

SARGASSO SEA – EUROPE

ARCTIC CIRCLE – ANTARCTICA

Bering Sea

CANADA

Monarch butterfly

MEXICO – ARCTIC

USA

MEXICO – USA

Sargasso Sea

Atlantic Ocean

MEXICO

Grey whales can migrate up to **20,000 km** in a year.

Grey Whale

Pacific Ocean

Arctic terns migrate **70,000 km** every year. In its lifetime a single tern will fly **three times the distance to the Moon.**

Arctic Tern

KEY

Ocean routes

Air routes

Land routes

Weddell Sea

Southern Ocean

Zooplankton

Every day, huge numbers of tiny animals called zooplankton (right), travel hundreds of metres up and down the ocean in search of food, in a movement called vertical migration.

Wandering glider dragonflies migrate by using fast-moving winds that blow **at altitudes of nearly 6.5 km.**

A single leatherback turtle swam more than **20,500 km from Indonesia to America** in 2003.

A European eel will migrate to breed and lay up to **10 million eggs at once.**

Wandering glider dragonfly

Leatherback Turtle

55

Wildebeest

INDIA

INDIA – AFRICA

Indian Ocean

INDONESIA

CHRISTMAS ISLAND

AUSTRALIA

KENYA

TANZANIA

Nearly **1.5 million wildebeest** take part in the **largest land migration on the planet.**

Red crab

On Christmas Island near Indonesia, nearly **50 million red crabs** migrate to the sea at the same time to lay eggs.

ANTARCTICA

Living in
CITIES

Since the earliest cities were founded more than 10,000 years ago, more and more people have been moving to live in urban settlements. This movement of people from the country to cities is called urbanisation.

PEOPLE LIVING IN URBAN AREAS
AND CITIES WITH MORE THAN 10 MILLION PEOPLE

This map shows the percentage of people that live in towns and cities in each country around the world.

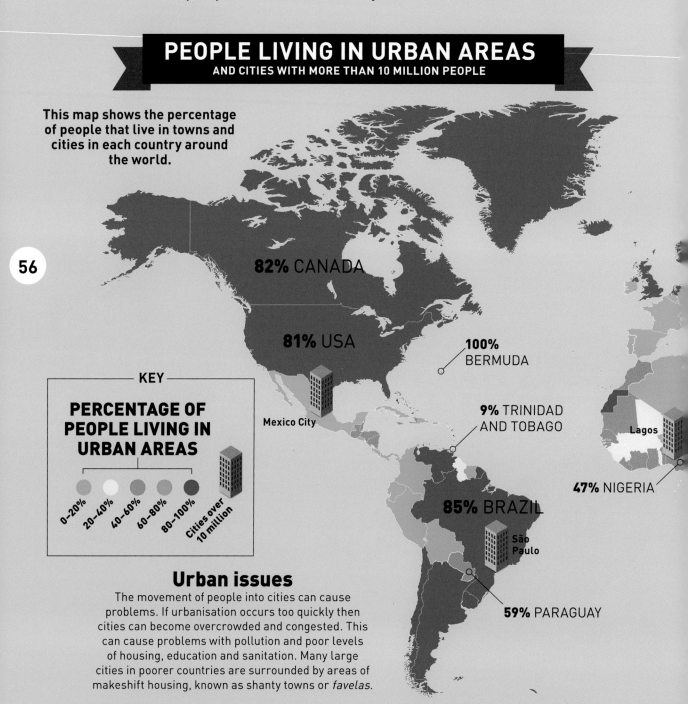

82% CANADA

81% USA

100% BERMUDA

Mexico City

KEY

PERCENTAGE OF PEOPLE LIVING IN URBAN AREAS

0-20% 20-40% 40-60% 60-80% 80-100% Cities over 10 million

9% TRINIDAD AND TOBAGO

Lagos

47% NIGERIA

85% BRAZIL

São Paulo

59% PARAGUAY

Urban issues

The movement of people into cities can cause problems. If urbanisation occurs too quickly then cities can become overcrowded and congested. This can cause problems with pollution and poor levels of housing, education and sanitation. Many large cities in poorer countries are surrounded by areas of makeshift housing, known as shanty towns or *favelas*.

CHANGES IN LEVELS OF URBANISATION (%)

	WORLD	AFRICA	ASIA	EUROPE	LATIN AMERICA AND CARIBBEAN	NORTHERN AMERICA	OCEANIA	
1950	29.6	14.0	17.5	51.1	41.3	63.9	62.4	1950
2000	46.6	34.5	37.5	70.9	75.3	79.1	70.5	2000
2050	66.4	55.9	64.2	82.0	86.2	87.4	73.5	2050

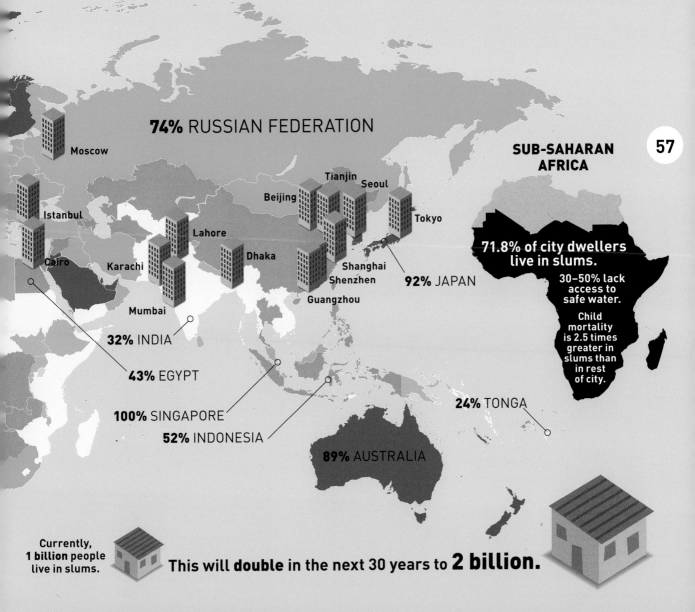

57

74% RUSSIAN FEDERATION

Moscow

Istanbul

Cairo

Karachi

Lahore

Dhaka

Mumbai

Beijing

Tianjin

Seoul

Tokyo

Shanghai
Shenzhen

Guangzhou

92% JAPAN

32% INDIA

43% EGYPT

100% SINGAPORE

52% INDONESIA

89% AUSTRALIA

24% TONGA

SUB-SAHARAN AFRICA

71.8% of city dwellers live in slums.

30–50% lack access to safe water.

Child mortality is 2.5 times greater in slums than in rest of city.

Currently, **1 billion people** live in slums.

This will **double** in the next 30 years to **2 billion.**

Water
ACCESS

Water is vital to humans, and we use 4,000 cubic km of it ever year – that's more water than in Lake Huron, USA. We drink it to stay alive, it irrigates our crops and it is used in all types of industry. However, not everyone on the planet has access to clean, safe water.

FRESHWATER ACCESS

While some countries have access to plenty of water, others have problems making sure that all of their people get enough water. This map shows the levels of water that are naturally present in each country and the countries with the largest populations who cannot get water that is safe to drink and free from contamination.

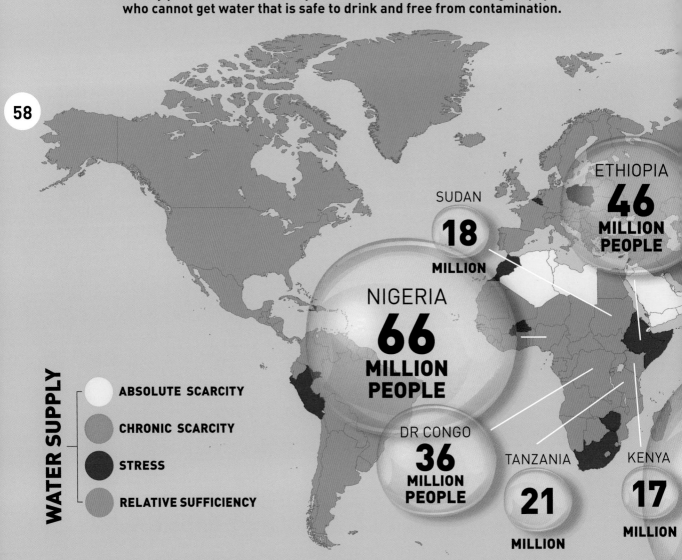

WATER SUPPLY

- ABSOLUTE SCARCITY
- CHRONIC SCARCITY
- STRESS
- RELATIVE SUFFICIENCY

ETHIOPIA
46 MILLION PEOPLE

SUDAN
18 MILLION

NIGERIA
66 MILLION PEOPLE

DR CONGO
36 MILLION PEOPLE

TANZANIA
21 MILLION

KENYA
17 MILLION

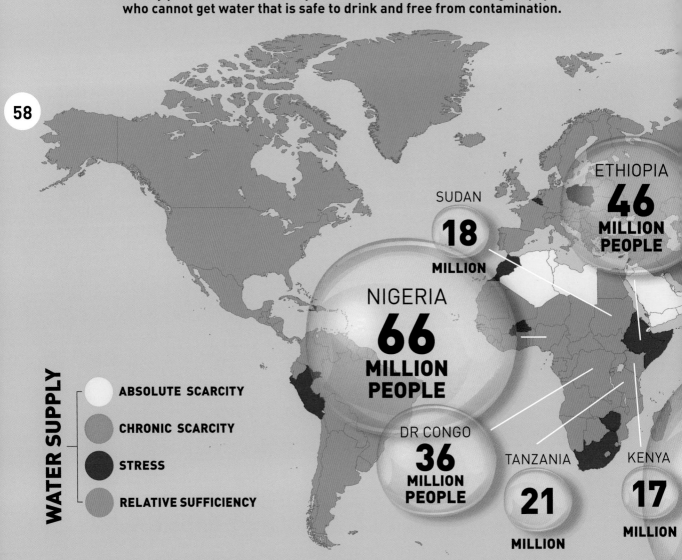

Sanitation

A reliable way of removing and treating human waste is essential to provide safe drinking water and prevent the spread of disease. People living in countries without these services are prone to diseases such as cholera, diarrhoea and typhoid.

2.5 BILLION PEOPLE AROUND THE WORLD DO NOT HAVE ACCESS TO ADEQUATE SANITATION FACILITIES.

CHINA
119 MILLION PEOPLE

BANGLADESH
28 MILLION

INDONESIA
43 MILLION PEOPLE

INDIA
97 MILLION PEOPLE

7 BILLION
6 BILLION
5 BILLION
4 BILLION
3 BILLION
2 BILLION
1 BILLION

THAT'S OVER 35% OF THE WORLD

Diseases and
DOCTORS

Death from disease is a constant threat in any part of the world.
Key to fighting disease is a country's health service and the
number of doctors and facilities available.

MOST LIKELY CAUSES OF DEATH

**This world map shows the
diseases and conditions
that cause the greatest
number of deaths
in each country.**

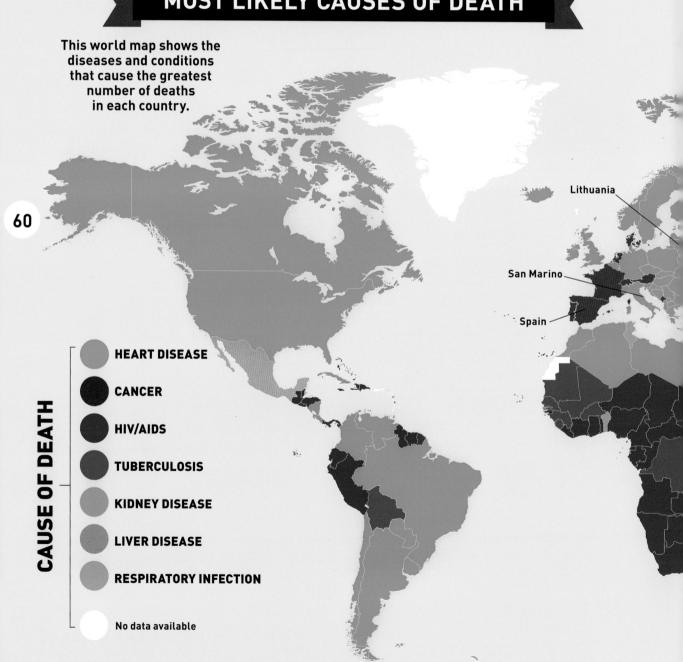

60

Lithuania

San Marino

Spain

CAUSE OF DEATH

- HEART DISEASE
- CANCER
- HIV/AIDS
- TUBERCULOSIS
- KIDNEY DISEASE
- LIVER DISEASE
- RESPIRATORY INFECTION

No data available

DISEASE AND WEALTH

The wealth of a country can decide the diseases its people are most susceptible to. People living in poorer countries are more likely to die from infectious diseases, because their countries have fewer doctors and health facilities. People in richer countries are more likely to die from conditions caused by bad habits, such as smoking.

Lower respiratory infections

91

Diarrhoeal diseases

53

Top 3 causes of death in low-income countries
(deaths per 100,000)

HIV/AIDS

65

Top 3 causes of death in high-income countries
(deaths per 100,000)

Stroke

95

Trachea, bronchus, lung cancers

49

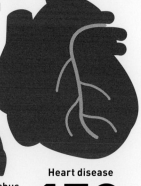

Heart disease

158

Georgia

Bhutan

Laos

Qatar

Cambodia

Indonesia

Mozambique

61

Doctors

Countries with a high number of doctors are likely to have a good standard of healthcare, helping to prevent and control diseases. According to the World Health Organisation, fewer than 2.3 health workers (doctors, nurses and midwives) per 1,000 people is not enough to meet healthcare needs. These figures show how many doctors there are for every 1,000 people.

--- LOWEST ---

Mozambique 0.1

Laos 0.2
Indonesia 0.2
Cambodia 0.2
Bhutan 0.3

--- HIGHEST ---

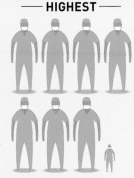

Qatar 7.7 doctors per 1,000 people

San Marino 5.1
Georgia 4.2
Lithuania 4.1
Spain 3.7

A LONG LIFE?

Today, the average life expectancy around the world is 70, with men living an average of 68 years and women 73 years. How long you live depends on how wealthy you are, whether or not you have access to sanitation (including a toilet!) and the quality of your diet.

AVERAGE AGES

The richer a country is, and the more its population earns – measured in Gross Domestic Product (GDP) per person – the longer its population usually lives.

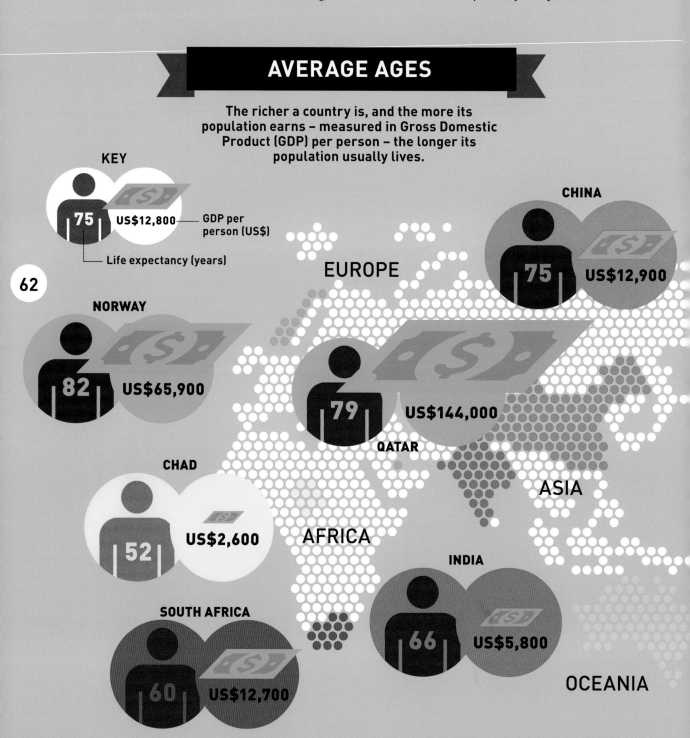

KEY

75 — Life expectancy (years)

US$12,800 — GDP per person (US$)

EUROPE

62

NORWAY
82 US$65,900

CHINA
75 US$12,900

79 US$144,000
QATAR

ASIA

CHAD
52 US$2,600

AFRICA

INDIA
66 US$5,800

SOUTH AFRICA
60 US$12,700

OCEANIA

KEEP IT CLEAN

Countries with good sanitation are able to get rid of human waste cleanly and effectively. This can prevent the spread of fatal diseases and increases the life expectancy, allowing people to live longer, healthier lives.

Every 20 seconds
a child dies as a result of poor sanitation.

1990 **49%**   2010 **63%**   2015 **67%**

Access to sanitation (% of world population)

Access to sanitation (% of country's population)

SOUTH SUDAN **16%**   KENYA **31%**

INDONESIA **71%**   PANAMA **80%**   GERMANY **100%**

The World Bank lists 38 countries whose people have 100% access to improved sanitation facilities. These include the USA, the UK, Greenland, Saudi Arabia, Australia and South Korea.

NORTH AMERICA

USA
79   US$54,800

AUSTRALIA
83   US$46,600

HAITI
63   US$1,800

SOUTH AMERICA

AFRICA 59 (male 58, female 60)
ASIA 71 (male 69, female 73)
SOUTH AMERICA 75 (male 71, female 78)
NORTH AMERICA 79 (male 77, female 81)
OCEANIA 77 (male 75, female 79)
EUROPE 78 (male 74, female 81)

Average life expectancy by region (in years)

Getting HEAVY

Obesity is a problem in many parts of the world, with more than one-third of the people in some countries being extremely overweight. This is the result of eating too much and eating foods that are high in calories.

LEVELS OF OBESITY

This map shows the percentages of household income spent on food in different countries around the world and the levels of obesity. In general, wealthier countries spend a smaller percentage on food, but have higher levels of obesity.

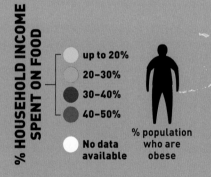

% HOUSEHOLD INCOME SPENT ON FOOD

- up to 20%
- 20–30%
- 30–40%
- 40–50%
- No data available

% population who are obese

What is obesity?

How overweight a person is is measured using their body mass index (BMI). This compares their mass with their height and is calculated using the following equation:

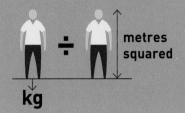

kg ÷ metres squared

According to the World Health Organisation, a BMI of 25 or more means a person is overweight, and a BMI of 30 or more means a person is obese.

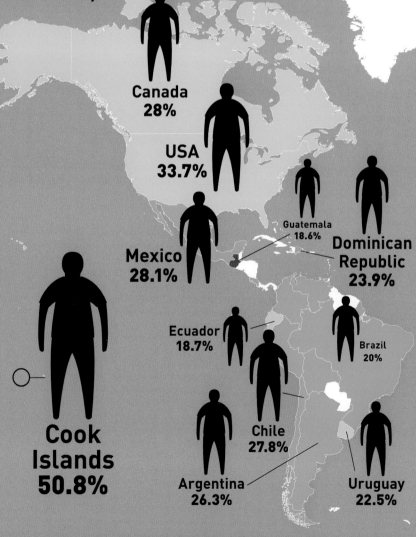

Canada
28%

USA
33.7%

Guatemala
18.6%

Dominican
Republic
23.9%

Mexico
28.1%

Ecuador
18.7%

Brazil
20%

Chile
27.8%

Cook
Islands
50.8%

Argentina
26.3%

Uruguay
22.5%

OBESITY AND CALORIES

How much you should eat depends on your age, metabolism and how active you are, but adult men should eat 2,500 calories a day on average and women should eat about 2,000 calories a day.

% of population that are obese ⟷

Average calories eaten per day ↕

India **2,300**
3.2%

Democratic Republic of Congo
1,590 1.9%

USA 3,770 kcal per day
32.6% citizens obese

UK **3,440**
26.9%

Argentina **3,000**
23.6%

These figures show how many calories people eat in each country, with the percentage of obese people living there.

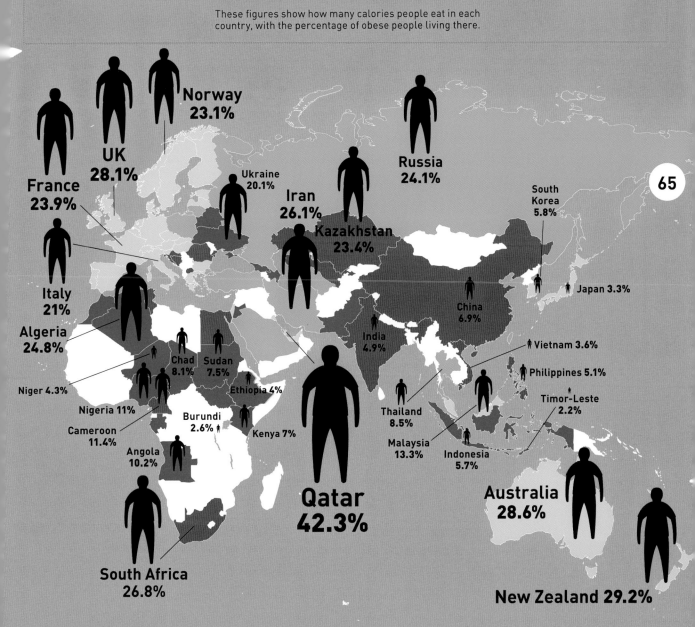

Norway
23.1%

UK
28.1%

France
23.9%

Italy
21%

Algeria
24.8%

Niger 4.3%

Nigeria 11%

Cameroon
11.4%

Angola
10.2%

South Africa
26.8%

Ukraine
20.1%

Iran
26.1%

Kazakhstan
23.4%

Russia
24.1%

South Korea
5.8%

Japan 3.3%

China
6.9%

India
4.9%

Vietnam 3.6%

Philippines 5.1%

Timor-Leste
2.2%

Thailand
8.5%

Malaysia
13.3%

Indonesia
5.7%

Chad
8.1%

Sudan
7.5%

Ethiopia 4%

Burundi
2.6%

Kenya 7%

Qatar
42.3%

Australia
28.6%

New Zealand **29.2%**

Food and
DRINK

People living in rich countries usually eat more than those living in poor nations. The ingredients of different national diets also vary, with some countries eating more meat, while others eat more vegetables.

DAILY DIETS AROUND THE WORLD

This map shows some of the highest and lowest average calorie intakes in countries around the world, as well as how many calories come from different types of food.

66

USA
3,641
469
504
1,342
799
527

MEXICO
3,021
329
335
772
1,302
283

BRAZIL
3,286
448
599
932
954
353

WORLD AVERAGE
2,870
272
497
570
1,296
235

KEY

Meat
Meat and fish

Grains
Rice, wheat and corn

Sugar/fat
Sugar and vegetable oil

Dairy/eggs
Eggs, milk and animal fats

Produce
Fruit, vegetables and pulses

Fast food frenzy

In a little over 50 years, McDonald's has increased in size from being a one-restaurant brand to...

36,525 restaurants **in** **119** countries **serving** **69 million** customers every single day.

Fast food outlets worldwide

McDonald's **36,525**

Subway **43,496**

KFC **19,952**

Pizza Hut **14,812**

Burger King **12,000**

Timeline

The first McDonald's restaurant opened in 1948 – it was called the 'McDonald's Bar-B-Q'.

The first franchise McDonald's opened in 1953.

1958 **34** restaurants	1965 **700**	1988 **10,000**	2005 **30,766**
1959 **100**	1968 **1,000**	1996 **20,000**	2009 **32,478**
1963 **500**	1978 **5,000**	1997 **23,000**	2015 **36,525**

489   655
869   **899**
501

UK **3,413**

353   588
801   **1,164**
452

RUSSIA **3,358**

509   605
338   **1,451**
170

CHINA **3,073**

67

97   451
206   **1,318**
31

NORTH KOREA **2,103**

122   89
419   **651**
414

SOMALIA **1,695**

29   366
471   **1,394**
198

INDIA **2,458**

553   516
985   708
505

AUSTRALIA **3,267**

Growing FOOD

In order to feed its population, a country can grow the food on farms, or import food from countries that produce an excess. However, some countries are too poor to buy all the food they need.

IMPORTERS AND EXPORTERS

This map shows the world's biggest importers and exporters of food produce in billions of US dollars per year. It also shows the countries with the largest proportion of undernourished people.

USA
$55.7 BN

UK
$36.3 BN

FRANCE
$45.3 BN

Imports

Exports

USA
$72.6 BN

Haiti

COUNTRIES WITH HIGHEST LEVELS OF UNDERNOURISHMENT
(PERCENTAGE OF POPULATION UNDERNOURISHED)

HAITI **52%**
ZAMBIA **48%**
CENTRAL AFRICAN REPUBLIC **38%**
NORTH KOREA **38%**
NAMIBIA **37%**

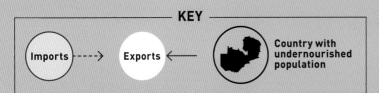

--- KEY ---

Imports ---->

Exports <----

Country with undernourished population

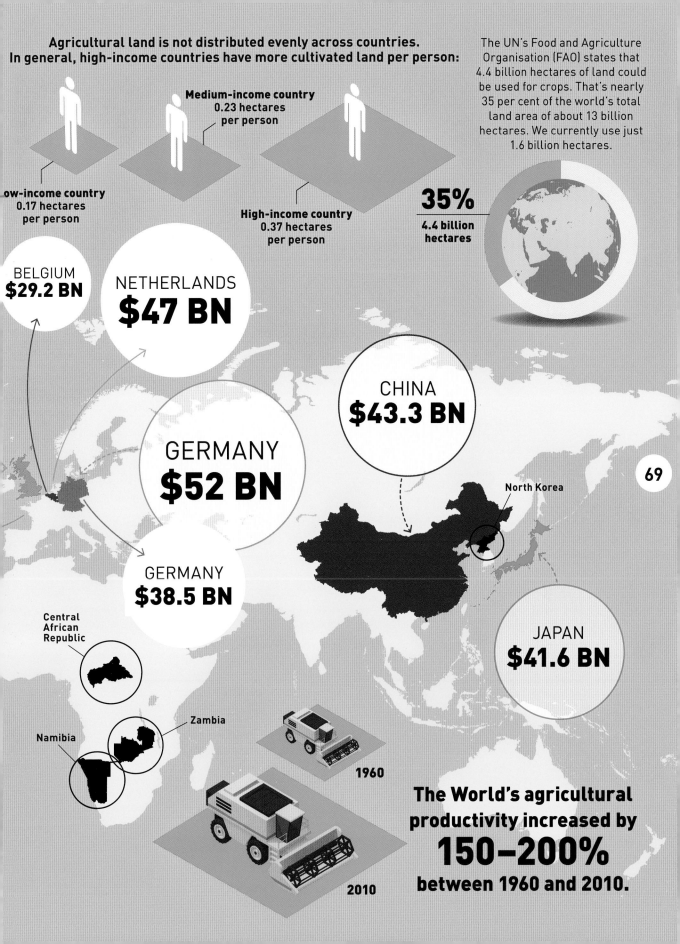

Agricultural land is not distributed evenly across countries. In general, high-income countries have more cultivated land per person:

Medium-income country
0.23 hectares per person

ow-income country
0.17 hectares per person

High-income country
0.37 hectares per person

The UN's Food and Agriculture Organisation (FAO) states that 4.4 billion hectares of land could be used for crops. That's nearly 35 per cent of the world's total land area of about 13 billion hectares. We currently use just 1.6 billion hectares.

35%
4.4 billion hectares

BELGIUM
$29.2 BN

NETHERLANDS
$47 BN

CHINA
$43.3 BN

GERMANY
$52 BN

North Korea

69

GERMANY
$38.5 BN

Central African Republic

JAPAN
$41.6 BN

Zambia

Namibia

1960

The World's agricultural productivity increased by
150–200%
between 1960 and 2010.

2010

TRADE

Which goods countries trade and ship to other nations depends on their accessibility to raw materials. Countries that are short in raw materials may choose to import them (ship them in) from countries that export them (ship them out) and use them to manufacture other goods.

HIGHEST VALUE EXPORT

This map shows the major type of export for each country in terms of the amount of money it earns.

TYPE OF EXPORT

- OIL AND GAS
- FOOD AND DRINK
- METALS AND MINERALS
- PRECIOUS METALS AND MINERALS
- TEXTILES AND CLOTHES
- MACHINERY AND TRANSPORTATION
- ELECTRONICS
- WOOD
- OTHER

Fish

Motor Vehicles and Parts

Capital Goods

Electrical Equipment
Machinery
Motor Vehicles
Diamonds
Fish
Manufactured Goods
Computers
Machinery
Engineering Products
Agricultural Products
Machinery
Clothing
Food
Uranium
Phosphates
Cotton
Natural Gas
Oil
Fish
Iron
Oil
Petroleum
Petroleum
Sugar
Aluminium
Transport Equipment
Diamonds
Cotton
Clothes and shoes
Petroleum
Rubber
Timber
Petroleum
Cocoa Beans
Oil
Petroleum
Copper
Transport Equipment
Diamonds
Oil
Natural Gas
Diamonds
Soybeans
Soybeans
Beef
Diamonds
Diamonds
Gold

IMPORT-EXPORT

China is the world's largest exporter because it has a large source of affordable labour and has developed a huge manufacturing industry. The USA is the world's largest importer because it is the wealthiest country in the world and its population demands goods that are made around the globe.

China **31.3**

USA **11.2**

Japan **5.7**

Top exporters of containerised cargo (TEUs millions)

Taiwan **3.4**

South Korea **5.2**

USA **17.6**

China **12.0**

Japan **6.1**

Top importers of containerised cargo (TEUs millions)

South Korea **4.5**

Germany **2.8**

Petroleum

Motor Vehicles

Oil

Clothes

Oil

Petroleum

Oil

Copper

Electronic Equipment and Machinery

Motor Vehicles

Minerals

Semi-conductors

Precious Stones

Opium

Textiles

Cement

Tea

Wood Products

Clothing

Coffee

Tea

Gold

Livestock

Tobacco

Coffee

Aluminium

Platinum

Soft Drink Concentrates

Electronic Equipment and Machinery

Oil and Gas

Machinery and Transportation Equipment

Coal

Sugar

Dairy Products

Shipping

71

The largest cargo ships can carry nearly 20,000 TEUs and are longer than four football pitches. Ninety per cent of world trade is carried by the international shipping industry. There are more than 50,000 ships in the world merchant fleet. They are registered with more than 150 countries and crewed by over 1 million sailors.

Wear it OUT

High fashion means big business. However, while most of the clothes we wear are made in some of the poorest countries, the money from sales flows to rich clothing companies who are based in the wealthiest nations.

WORLD'S MOST VALUABLE FASHION BRANDS

This map shows the value of the world's richest clothing brands and where they are located.

Ralph Lauren
USA
US$4.9 billion

Gap
USA
US$4.1 billion

Burberry
UK
US$5.6 billion

Tiffany
USA
US$5.9 billion

Nike
USA
US$19.8 billion

Louis Vuitton
France
US$22.5 billion

Chanel
France
US$7 billion

Hermès
France
US$9 billion

Cartier
France
US$7.4 billion

Zara
Spain
US$12.1 billion

FAIR PAY?

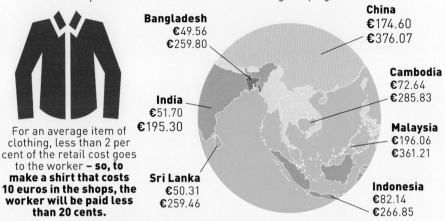

The Asia Floor Wage Alliance calculates what should be the minimum wage in countries that produce most of the world's clothes (bottom figure in euros) and compares it to the current minimum wage (top figure in euros):

Bangladesh
€49.56
€259.80

China
€174.60
€376.07

Cambodia
€72.64
€285.83

India
€51.70
€195.30

Malaysia
€196.06
€361.21

Sri Lanka
€50.31
€259.46

Indonesia
€82.14
€266.85

For an average item of clothing, less than 2 per cent of the retail cost goes to the worker – **so, to make a shirt that costs 10 euros in the shops, the worker will be paid less than 20 cents.**

H&M
Sweden
US$21 billion

Hugo Boss
Germany
US$4.1 billion

Adidas
Germany
US$7.4 billion

Prada
Italy
US$6 billion

Gucci
Italy
US$10.4 billion

Top 10 COTTON PRODUCING — nations —
(tonnes per year)

China 6,532,000
India 6,423,000
USA 3,553,000
Pakistan 2,308,000
Brazil 1,524,000
Uzbekistan 849,000
Turkey 697,000
Australia 501,000
Turkmenistan 332,000
Greece 297,000

Every year, China produces the same weight in cotton as 35,000 blue whales.

MONEY

There are about 180 different currencies in use around the world. These are currencies that are approved by governments and exchanged for goods and services. Other ways to pay include cryptocurrencies, such as bitcoin, which are not controlled by national banks or governments.

CURRENCIES AROUND THE WORLD

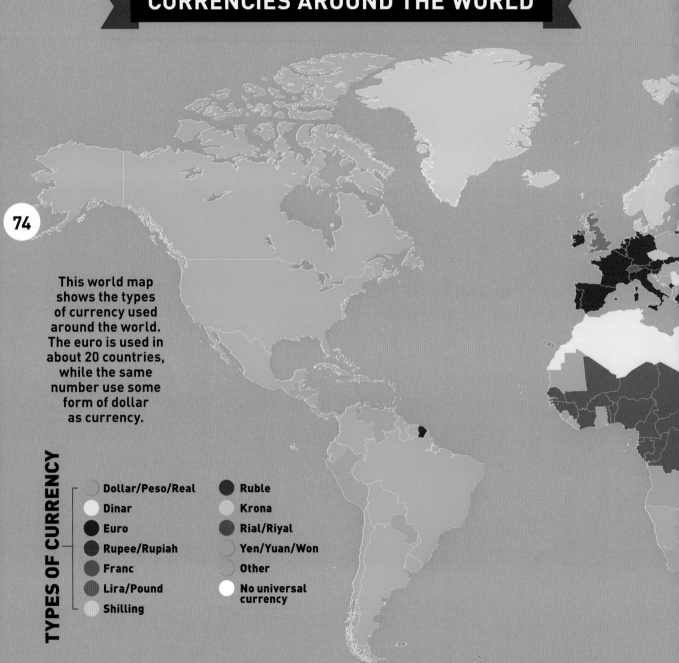

This world map shows the types of currency used around the world. The euro is used in about 20 countries, while the same number use some form of dollar as currency.

TYPES OF CURRENCY

- Dollar/Peso/Real
- Dinar
- Euro
- Rupee/Rupiah
- Franc
- Lira/Pound
- Shilling
- Ruble
- Krona
- Rial/Riyal
- Yen/Yuan/Won
- Other
- No universal currency

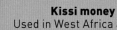

ANCIENT CURRENCIES

In the past, people around the world have used a wide range of objects and materials as currency, exchanging them for goods and services. These include salt, animal fur, metal objects and even massive stone wheels.

Kissi money
Used in West Africa around the end of the 19th century, these were T-shaped pieces of iron up to 40 cm long

Squirrel pelts
Used in medieval Russia

Katanga Cross
A copper cross weighing up to 1 kg and used in central Africa until the start of the 20th century

Rai stones
Huge stones measuring more than 3 m across, rai stones were used in Micronesia until the start of the 20th century

75

On 22 May 2010, Laszlo Hanyecz of the USA paid 10,000 bitcoins (about US$25) for 2 pizzas.

x10,000

Digital currency

Bitcoin is an online currency that can be used to buy a range of goods and services. It is not controlled by a bank or government and people can 'mine' or 'earn' bitcoins by using powerful computers to solve difficult maths problems. However, 65 per cent of all the bitcoins mined and bought are never used again – they are kept in 'inactive wallets'.

Today, as demand for bitcoins has soared, 10,000 bitcoins would be worth **£4 million.**

On the
LINE

How people communicate with each other varies from one country to the next. While those living in some countries can use large networks of fixed landlines, other countries do not have this infrastructure and their people tend to use mobile phones.

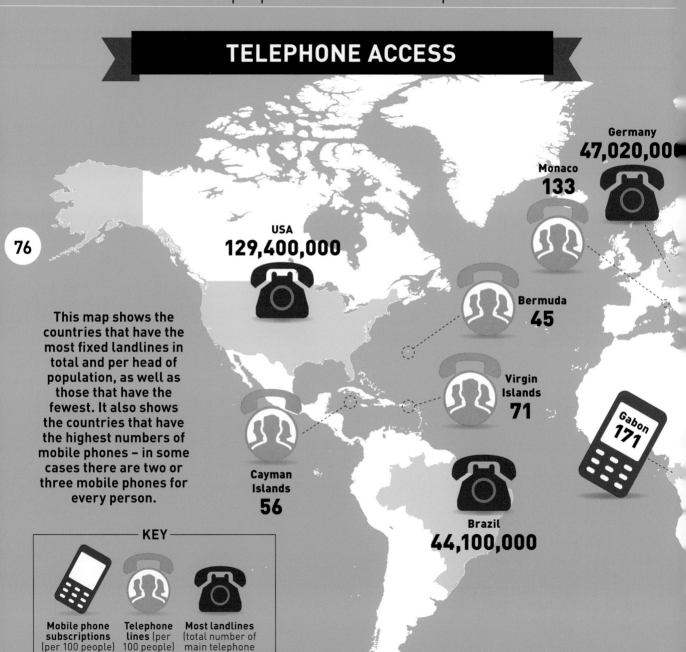

TELEPHONE ACCESS

This map shows the countries that have the most fixed landlines in total and per head of population, as well as those that have the fewest. It also shows the countries that have the highest numbers of mobile phones – in some cases there are two or three mobile phones for every person.

Germany
47,020,000

Monaco
133

USA
129,400,000

Bermuda
45

Virgin Islands
71

Gabon
171

Cayman Islands
56

Brazil
44,100,000

KEY

Mobile phone subscriptions (per 100 people)

Telephone lines (per 100 people)

Most landlines (total number of main telephone lines)

Phone calls

By far the greatest number of phone calls are short-distance calls made between places inside the same country. However, the busiest international phone lines are those running from the USA to Mexico and India. They are most likely used by people living abroad and phoning their friends and families at home.

Mexico **USA** **India**

LANDLINES VS. MOBILE PHONES

In the year up to June 2014, UK users spent 3 billion fewer minutes on fixed-line phones than they did the year before, a reduction of 12.7 per cent. During the same period, the time spent using mobile phones increased by 2.3 per cent.

12.7% 2.3%

Japan
63,610,000

China
249,400,000

Kuwait
218

Macao
323

Hong Kong
234

Hong Kong
61

Maldives
189

THERE ARE ABOUT
3.8 BILLION MOBILE PHONE SUBSCRIBERS AROUND THE WORLD.

Internet
ACCESS

Since the creation of the internet, how we access the worldwide web has changed. Instead of using a computer on a desk, people are now tending to use smaller devices, such as tablets and smartphones, accessing the internet while they are on the move.

INTERNET USAGE

KEY

Countries with the most number of personal computer users

Countries where the greatest percentage of the population uses tablet computers

Countries with the highest number of internet users per 100 people

Countries where the greatest percentage of the population owns a smartphone

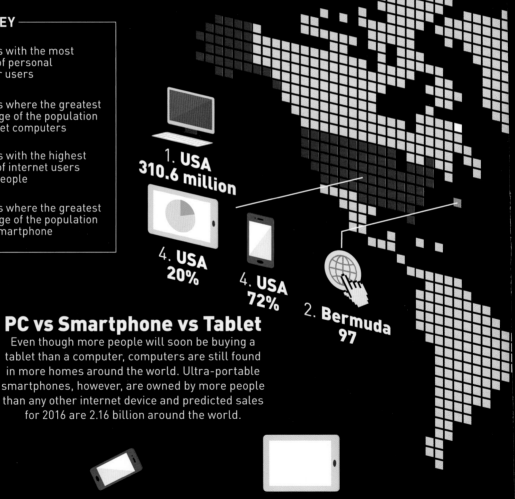

1. **USA** 310.6 million

4. **USA** 20%

4. **USA** 72%

2. **Bermuda** 97

PC vs Smartphone vs Tablet

Even though more people will soon be buying a tablet than a computer, computers are still found in more homes around the world. Ultra-portable smartphones, however, are owned by more people than any other internet device and predicted sales for 2016 are 2.16 billion around the world.

17%
Percentage of world population that owns a computer

27%
Percentage of world population that owns a smartphone

13.5%
Percentage of world population that owns a tablet

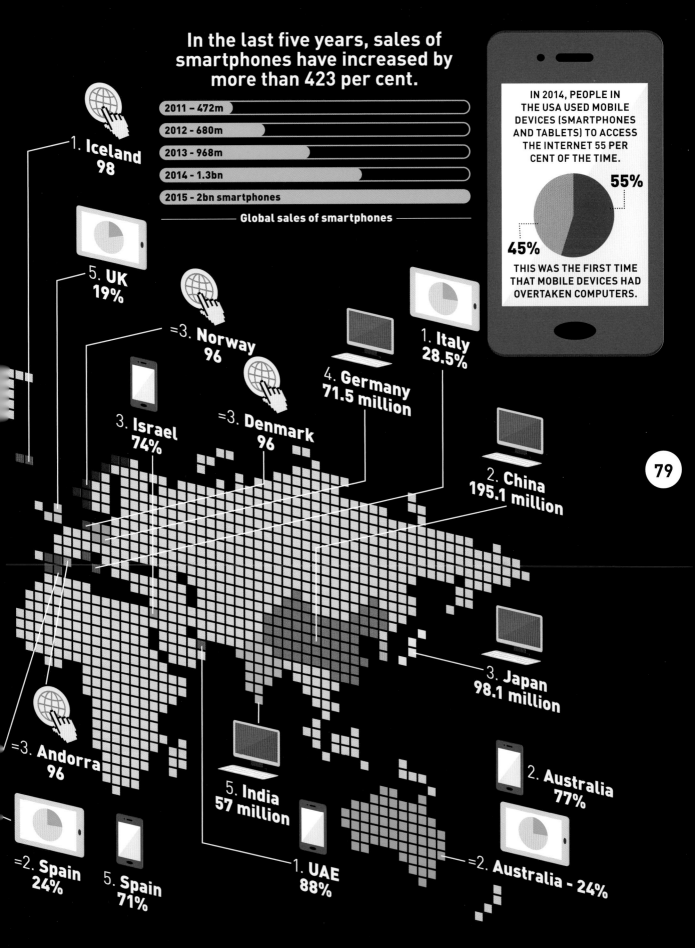

In the last five years, sales of smartphones have increased by more than 423 per cent.

2011 – 472m
2012 – 680m
2013 – 968m
2014 – 1.3bn
2015 – 2bn smartphones

Global sales of smartphones

IN 2014, PEOPLE IN THE USA USED MOBILE DEVICES (SMARTPHONES AND TABLETS) TO ACCESS THE INTERNET 55 PER CENT OF THE TIME.

55%

45%

THIS WAS THE FIRST TIME THAT MOBILE DEVICES HAD OVERTAKEN COMPUTERS.

1. Iceland
98

5. UK
19%

=3. Norway
96

4. Germany
71.5 million

1. Italy
28.5%

3. Israel
74%

=3. Denmark
96

2. China
195.1 million

79

3. Japan
98.1 million

=3. Andorra
96

2. Australia
77%

5. India
57 million

=2. Spain
24%

5. Spain
71%

1. UAE
88%

=2. Australia - 24%

Social
MEDIA

Social media allows people to chat and share images with others all over the world. However, no single social network is yet fully global. Russian and Chinese speakers, for example, use large local networks of their own.

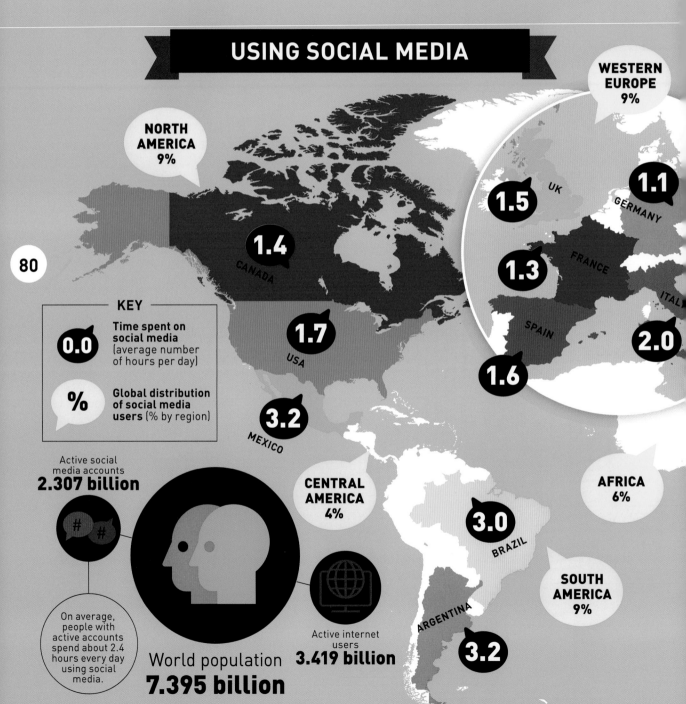

USING SOCIAL MEDIA

WESTERN EUROPE 9%

NORTH AMERICA 9%

1.5 UK
1.1 GERMANY
1.4 CANADA
1.3 FRANCE
ITALY
1.7 USA
SPAIN
1.6
2.0

KEY

0.0 — Time spent on social media (average number of hours per day)

% — Global distribution of social media users (% by region)

3.2 MEXICO

Active social media accounts
2.307 billion

\# \#

CENTRAL AMERICA 4%

3.0 BRAZIL

AFRICA 6%

SOUTH AMERICA 9%

On average, people with active accounts spend about 2.4 hours every day using social media.

Active internet users
3.419 billion

World population
7.395 billion

ARGENTINA
3.2

Global
LANGUAGES

There are more than 7,000 languages spoken around the world. Some of the most popular, such as Mandarin and Hindi, are spoken in countries with huge populations, while others, including English and Spanish, are widely spoken because of the colonial history of their original countries.

MAJOR LANGUAGES

This map shows what the major language is in each country in the world.

82

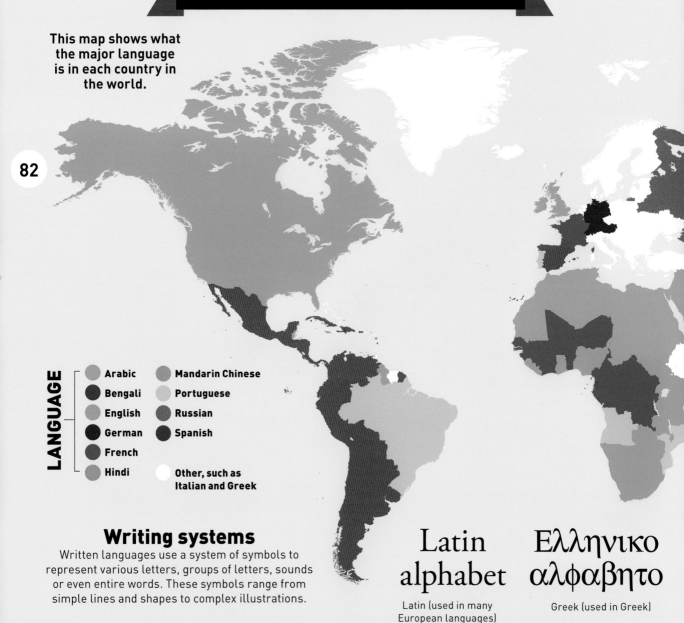

LANGUAGE
- Arabic
- Bengali
- English
- German
- French
- Hindi
- Mandarin Chinese
- Portuguese
- Russian
- Spanish
- Other, such as Italian and Greek

Writing systems
Written languages use a system of symbols to represent various letters, groups of letters, sounds or even entire words. These symbols range from simple lines and shapes to complex illustrations.

Latin
alphabet

Latin (used in many European languages)

Ελληνικο
αλφαβητο

Greek (used in Greek)

LANGUAGES OF THE INTERNET

The large number of internet users in North America, the UK and Oceania means that English is by far the most common language used to search the internet.

Languages of Internet users (millions of users)

ENGLISH	800.6
CHINESE	649.4
SPANISH	222.4
ARABIC	135.6
PORTUGUESE	121.8
JAPANESE	109.6
RUSSIAN	87.5
GERMAN	81.1
FRENCH	78.9
MALAYSIAN	75.5

Most popular languages

At one point in its history, the British Empire covered almost one-third of the globe. This is why today English is spoken in more countries than any other language. Other former empires include Portugal, France and Spain, and their languages are spoken around the world, while Arabic dominates nations in northern Africa and the Middle East.

83

Portuguese
11

French
51

Arabic
59

English
101
countries

Russian
11

Spanish
31

Кириллица алфавит

Cyrillic (used in Russian)

日本語の漢字

Kanji (used in Japanese)

Holiday
TIME

Key factors that affect how much time people spend on holiday and where they go include cost, the amount of holidays they can have and what their own country has to offer in terms of facilities and climate.

MOST POPULAR DESTINATIONS

These figures show how many foreign tourists visit each of these countries every year and the most popular tourist attractions.

Most visited attraction **Notre Dame Cathedral, Paris**

FRANCE 84,726,000 **1**

USA 69,768,000 **2**

Most visited attraction **Times Square, New York City**

Most visited attraction **Alhambra Palace, Granada**

SPAIN 60,661,000 **3**

ITALY 47,704,000 **5**

Most visited attraction **St. Peter's Basilica, Vatican City**

TAKING TIME OFF

These figures show the countries that guarantee their
workers the highest and lowest amount of paid holiday.

38	AUSTRIA
35	PORTUGAL
34	SPAIN, GERMANY
31	ITALY, FRANCE
30	BELGIUM, NEW ZEALAND
28	AUSTRALIA
25	BRAZIL
19	CANADA

**Countries with the
most time off** (days)

**Countries with the
least time off** (days)

10	JAPAN
5	CHINA
0	USA

Tourist money

Tourists and holiday makers can bring
a lot of money into a country. These figures show
which countries earn the most from tourism.

85

Earnings from tourism
(US$ billions per year)

4 CHINA 55,686,000

Most visited attraction
**Forbidden City,
Beijing**

ITALY US$41.2

CHINA US$50

FRANCE US$53.6

SPAIN US$55.9

USA US$126.2

Carnivals and FESTIVALS

Every year, people gather together in huge celebrations. The largest of these celebrations are for religious reasons and may involve people making special journeys, called pilgrimages, to places they believe to be holy.

THE WORLD'S BIGGEST FESTIVALS

The word 'carnival' is thought to come from the Latin phrase *carne vale*, which means 'goodbye meat'. It refers to the last chance for Christians to eat meat before the fasting period of Lent. Many carnivals today are still held before Lent, while others, such as those in London and Toronto, are held later in the year and are celebrations of other cultures.

Haridwar
Allahabad
Manila
Ujjain
Nashik
Karbala
Mecca
Rio de Janeiro

LARGEST RELIGIOUS GATHERINGS

WORLD YOUTH DAY
Roman Catholic youth festival held every two to three years.
In 2013, 3.7 million attended in Rio de Janeiro, Brazil.

HAJJ
Annual Islamic pilgrimage to Mecca in Saudi Arabia.
3.2 million in 2012.

KUMBH MELA
Hindu pilgrimage held every three years in the Indian cities of Haridwar, Allahabad, Nashik and Ujjain.
Attended by 30 million in 2013.

ARBAEEN
Muslim pilgrimage held every year in Karbala, Iraq.
Attended by 17 million people in 2014.

POPE FRANCIS
On 18 January 2015, the Eucharistic Celebration of his five-day Philippine tour was held in Manila.
Attended by an estimated 6–7 million people.

Mardi Gras

New Orleans, USA
Shrove Tuesday
1,200,000

Carnevale

Venice, Italy
Shrove Tuesday
30,000

Carnival

Port of Spain,
Trinidad and Tobago
Sunday before Ash Wednesday
300,000

Carnival

Notting Hill, London, UK
Last weekend in August
1,600,000

Carnaval

Tenerife, Spain
Shrove Tuesday
250,000

Karneval

Cologne, Germany
Rosenmontag
1,000,000

Carnival

Rio de Janeiro, Brazil
Friday before Ash Wednesday
2,000,000

Intruz

Goa, India
*Saturday before
Ash Wednesday*
200,000

Carnival

Barranquilla, Colombia
*Saturday before
Ash Wednesday*
1,000,000

Caribana

Toronto, Canada
First weekend in August
1,300,000

RELIGION

More than 80 per cent of the world's population, or 5.8 billion people, are members of a religion. Of these 5.8 billion, 2.2 billion are Christian, 1.6 billion are Muslim, 1 billion are Hindu, 500 million are Buddhist and 14 million are Jewish.

MAJOR RELIGIONS

This map shows which religion is worshipped by the majority of people in each country around the world.

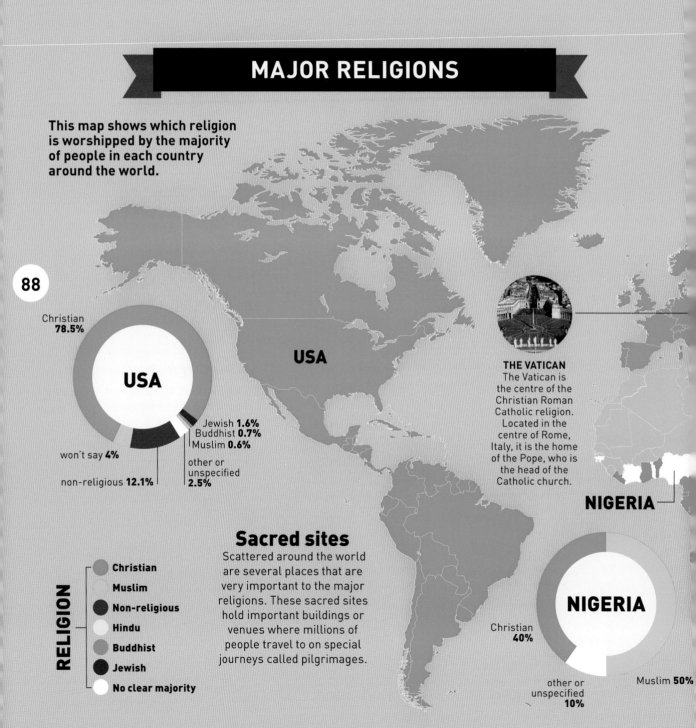

USA

USA
Christian **78.5%**
Jewish **1.6%**
Buddhist **0.7%**
Muslim **0.6%**
other or unspecified **2.5%**
won't say **4%**
non-religious **12.1%**

THE VATICAN
The Vatican is the centre of the Christian Roman Catholic religion. Located in the centre of Rome, Italy, it is the home of the Pope, who is the head of the Catholic church.

NIGERIA

Sacred sites
Scattered around the world are several places that are very important to the major religions. These sacred sites hold important buildings or venues where millions of people travel to on special journeys called pilgrimages.

RELIGION
- Christian
- Muslim
- Non-religious
- Hindu
- Buddhist
- Jewish
- No clear majority

NIGERIA
Christian **40%**
other or unspecified **10%**
Muslim **50%**

JERUSALEM, ISRAEL/WEST BANK
The city of Jerusalem is a sacred site for three major religions: Judaism, Christianity and Islam.

AMRITSAR, INDIA
The Golden Temple, or Harmandir Sahib, at Amritsar in India is the centre of the Sikh religion.

MECCA, SAUDI ARABIA
Every year, millions of Muslims make a pilgrimage, or Hajj, to Mecca, Saudi Arabia. Mecca is the birthplace of the prophet Muhammad and the holiest city in the religion of Islam.

VARANASI, INDIA
Located on the banks of the Ganges river, Varanasi is one of the most sacred sites in Hinduism. Millions of people come to the city to bathe in the river's holy waters.

SIZE OF RELIGIOUS GROUPS
% of the global population

- Jewish **0.2%**
- Other **6.7%**
- Buddhist **7.1%**
- Hindu **15%**
- Unaffiliated **16.3%**
- Muslim **23.2%**
- Christian **31.5%**

89

BODH GAYA, INDIA
Said to be the spot where Gautama Buddha achieved enlightenment, Bodh Gaya is a sacred pilgrimage site to members of the Buddhist religion.

INDIA

INDONESIA

Muslim **87.2%**

INDONESIA

Hindu **1.7%**

Christian **9.8%**

other or unspecified **1.3%**

Hindu **80.5%**

INDIA

Muslim **13.4%**

Christian **2.3%**

other or unspecified **1.9%**

Sikh **1.9%**

World of FOOTBALL

Football is the world's most popular sport, with approximately 250 million players, amateur and professional, and 1.3 billion followers in more than 200 countries.

THE BEAUTIFUL GAME

This map shows the countries with the most football players, as well as the locations of the world's richest clubs and largest stadiums.

ENGLAND
Wembley Stadium, London
90,000

SPAIN
Camp Nou Barcelona
99,786

Countries with the greatest number of football clubs

England 42,490 clubs

Brazil 29,208 clubs

Germany 26,837 clubs

UNITED STATES
The Rose Bowl, Pasadena
92,542

USA 24,472,778 players

ALGERIA
Stade 5 Juillet 1962, Algiers
85,000

France 20,062 clubs

Spain 18,190 clubs

Italy 16,697 clubs

MEXICO
Estadio Azteca, Mexico City
105,500

Brazil 13,197,733 players

KEY

Players
Five countries with the highest number of professional and amateur players

Richest
World's richest football clubs (total worth)

Stadiums
The largest stadiums and their capacity

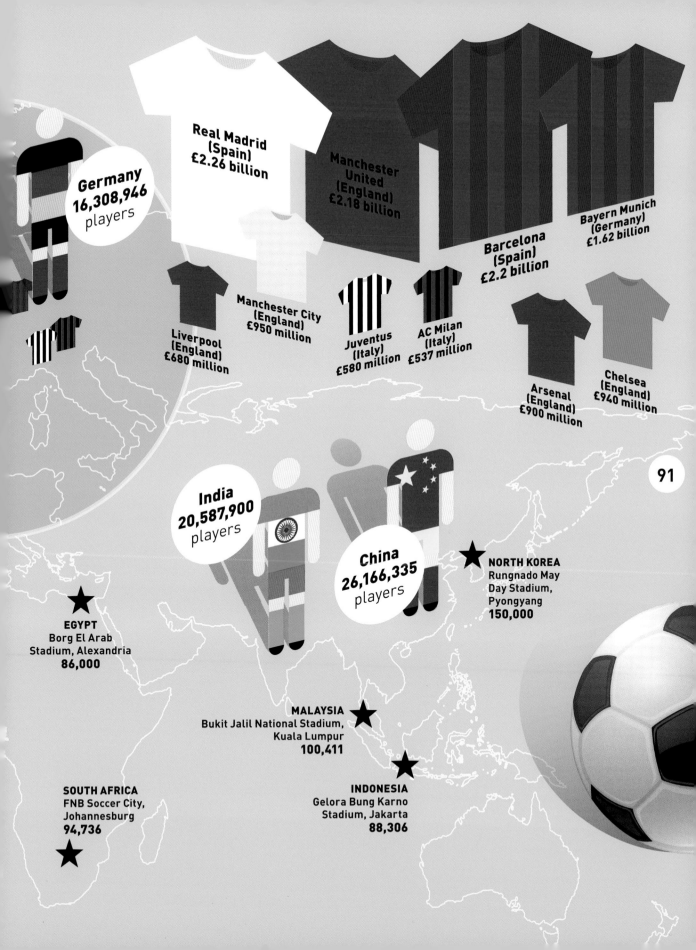

Real Madrid (Spain) £2.26 billion

Manchester United (England) £2.18 billion

Barcelona (Spain) £2.2 billion

Bayern Munich (Germany) £1.62 billion

Germany 16,308,946 players

Manchester City (England) £950 million

Liverpool (England) £680 million

Juventus (Italy) £580 million

AC Milan (Italy) £537 million

Arsenal (England) £900 million

Chelsea (England) £940 million

India 20,587,900 players

China 26,166,335 players

NORTH KOREA Rungnado May Day Stadium, Pyongyang 150,000

EGYPT Borg El Arab Stadium, Alexandria 86,000

MALAYSIA Bukit Jalil National Stadium, Kuala Lumpur 100,411

SOUTH AFRICA FNB Soccer City, Johannesburg 94,736

INDONESIA Gelora Bung Karno Stadium, Jakarta 88,306

The Olympic GAMES

Every four years, thousands of athletes gather to compete in the Summer and Winter Olympic games. So far, the USA has won the most bronze, silver and gold medals at the Summer Olympics with a total of 2,400.

SUMMER AND WINTER MEDALS

NORWAY 118

1994
1952

GREAT BRITAIN 10 236

1908
1948
2012

1928

193

1920

1936

1972

CANADA 62 59

1928
1948

1964
1976

1900

1924

2006

1992

1968

1956

2010

1988

1976

USA 96 976

1932
1980

FRANCE 202

1984

2002

1960

1996

1904

1992

1960

ITALY 198

1932
1984

1968

JAMAICA 17

This world map shows how successful countries around the world have been at both the Summer and Winter Olympics. It also locates the host cities for both games.

BRAZIL 23

2016

URUGUAY 2

KEY

Summer gold medals from selected countries around the world

Winter gold medals from selected countries around the world

Host Cities Summer Olympics

Host Cities Winter Olympics

Summary Games

Summer 🏅 Games   # Winter 🏅 Games

Summer Games

Greece, **Athens** 1896
France, **Paris** 1900
USA, **St Louis** 1904
UK, **London** 1908
Sweden, **Stockholm** 1912
Belgium, **Antwerp** 1920
France, **Paris** 1924
Netherlands, **Amsterdam** 1928
USA, **Los Angeles** 1932
Germany, **Berlin** 1936
UK, **London** 1948
Finland, **Helsinki** 1952
Australia, **Melbourne** 1956
Italy, **Rome** 1960
Japan, **Tokyo** 1964

Mexico, **Mexico City** 1968
Germany, **Munich** 1972
Canada, **Montreal** 1976
Soviet Union, **Moscow** 1980
USA, **Los Angeles** 1984
South Korea, **Seoul** 1988
Spain, **Barcelona** 1992
USA, **Atlanta** 1996
Australia, **Sydney** 2000
Greece, **Athens** 2004
China, **Beijing** 2008
UK, **London** 2012
Brazil, **Rio de Janeiro** 2016
Japan, **Tokyo** 2021

Winter Games

France, **Chamonix** 1924
Switzerland, **St Moritz** 1928
USA, **Lake Placid** 1932
Germany, **Garmisch-Partenkirchen** 1936
Switzerland, **St Moritz** 1948
Norway, **Oslo** 1952
Italy, **Cortina d'Ampezzo** 1956
USA, **Squaw Valley** 1960
Austria, **Innsbruck** 1964
France, **Grenoble** 1968
Japan, **Sapporo** 1972
Austria, **Innsbruck** 1976
USA, **Lake Placid** 1980
Yugoslavia, **Sarajevo** 1984

Canada, **Calgary** 1988
France, **Albertville** 1992
Norway, **Lillehammer** 1994
Japan, **Nagano** 1998
USA, **Salt Lake City** 2002
Italy, **Turin** 2006
Canada, **Vancouver** 2010
Russia, **Sochi** 2014
South Korea, **Pyeongchang** 2018
China, **Beijing** 2022

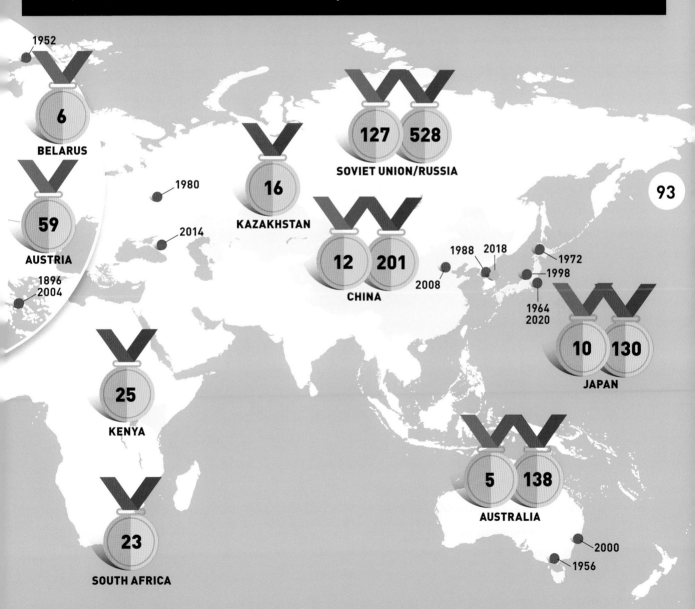

1952
6
BELARUS

59
AUSTRIA

1896
2004

1980

2014

16
KAZAKHSTAN

127 **528**
SOVIET UNION/RUSSIA

12 **201**
CHINA

2008
1988
2018
1972
1998
1964
2020

10 **130**
JAPAN

25
KENYA

23
SOUTH AFRICA

5 **138**
AUSTRALIA

2000
1956

93

The Silver
SCREEN

The production and screening of movies is a major global business, with the biggest blockbusters earning more than US$1 billion. Today, the industry stretches far beyond its traditional home of Hollywood.

NUMBER OF FEATURE FILMS PRODUCED

This map shows how many movies are made in countries around the world and the range of languages they are made in.

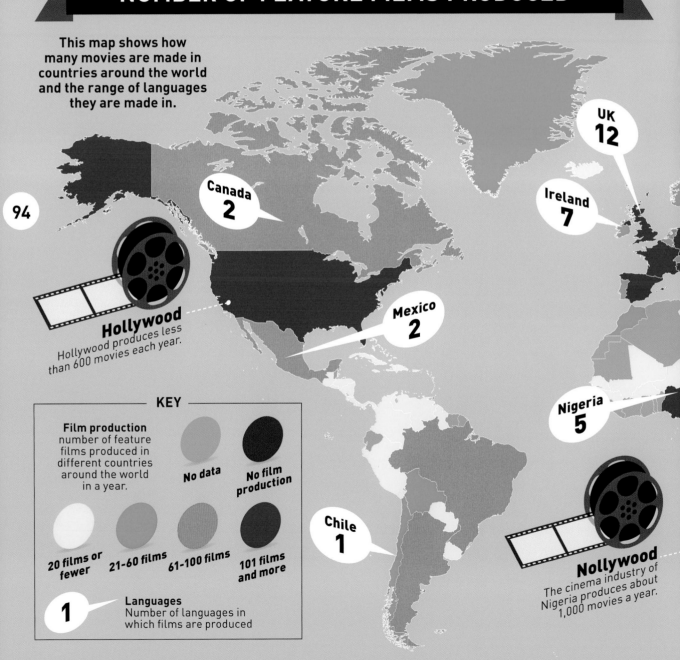

94

Canada
2

UK
12

Ireland
7

Hollywood
Hollywood produces less than 600 movies each year.

Mexico
2

Nigeria
5

Chile
1

Nollywood
The cinema industry of Nigeria produces about 1,000 movies a year.

KEY

Film production
number of feature films produced in different countries around the world in a year.

No data

No film production

20 films or fewer

21–60 films

61–100 films

101 films and more

1 Languages
Number of languages in which films are produced

CINEMA ADMISSIONS

While it only has the second-highest level of cinema admissions, the USA has the greatest share of global cinema earnings, taking more than US$10 billion a year, or about 30 per cent of the world's total.

Annual cinema admissions by country

India TICKET ADMIT **2.9 billion**

USA TICKET ADMIT **1.4 billion**

China TICKET ADMIT **264 million**

France TICKET ADMIT **201 million**

Mexico TICKET ADMIT **178 million**

Japan TICKET ADMIT **169 million**

UK TICKET ADMIT **173 million**

South Korea
157 million
Germany
136 million
Russia
132 million

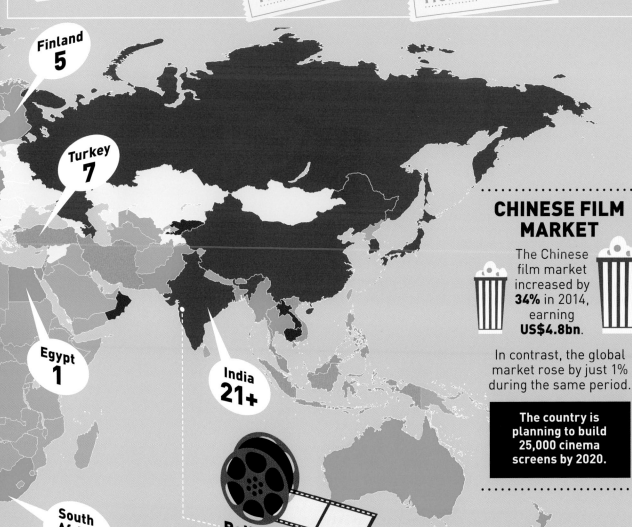

Finland
5

Turkey
7

Egypt
1

India
21+

South Africa
4

Bollywood
The Indian film industry makes more than 1,200 movies every year.

CHINESE FILM MARKET

The Chinese film market increased by **34%** in 2014, earning **US$4.8bn**.

In contrast, the global market rose by just 1% during the same period.

The country is planning to build 25,000 cinema screens by 2020.

Going for
A SONG

While music sales figures have stayed the same in recent years, how that music is sold has changed dramatically. Today, nearly half of all music earnings comes from digital formats, including downloads and streaming.

MUSIC SALES AND FESTIVALS

KEY

Music sales
Largest markets US$

Biggest music festivals
Total attendance

Canada
342 million

USA
4.89 billion

Digital revenues
45%

Recording industry earnings and where they come from

Global recorded music sales in 2015 totalled
US$15 BILLION

Physical format sales
39%

SUMMERFEST
(Wisconsin, USA)
840,000 in 2013

COACHELLA
(California)
675,000 in 2013

MAWAZINE
(Rabat, Morocco)
2.5 million in 2013

Brazil
246 million

ROCK IN RIO
(Brazil)
1,235,000 in 200?

Performance rights
14%

Synchronisation revenues (film, TV, advertising)
2%

Digital earnings

Buying and listening to tracks on the online has changed the music industry dramatically. In 2015, digital sales of music overtook physical sales for the first time, and the percentage of income made from digital sales is continuing to grow.

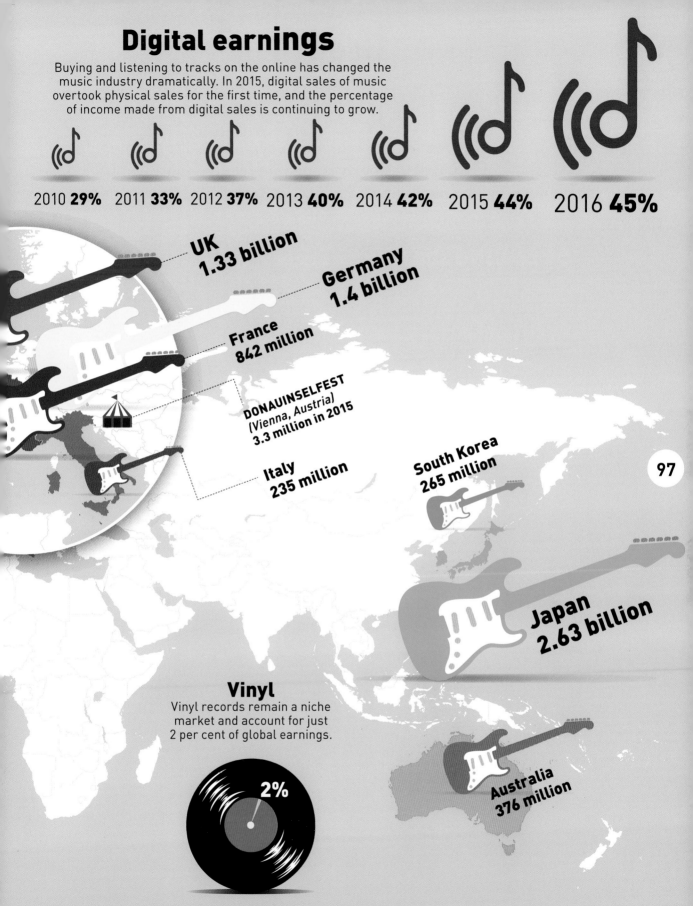

| 2010 **29%** | 2011 **33%** | 2012 **37%** | 2013 **40%** | 2014 **42%** | 2015 **44%** | 2016 **45%** |

UK
1.33 billion

Germany
1.4 billion

France
842 million

DONAUINSELFEST
(Vienna, Austria)
3.3 million in 2015

Italy
235 million

South Korea
265 million

Japan
2.63 billion

Vinyl
Vinyl records remain a niche market and account for just 2 per cent of global earnings.

2%

Australia
376 million

Great
MINDS

The amount a country invests in its education system is often reflected in its success in science and industry. However, people living in some of the poorest regions in the world usually have access to the least education.

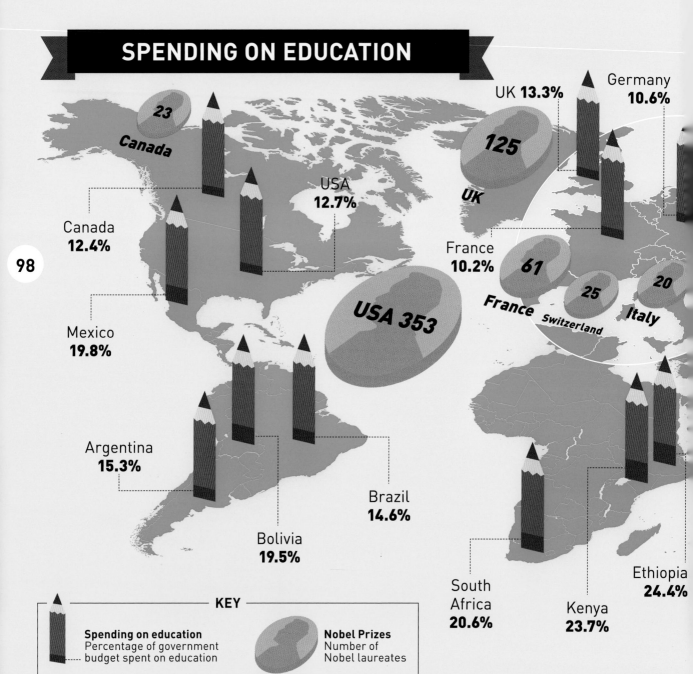

SPENDING ON EDUCATION

23
Canada

UK **13.3%**

Germany **10.6%**

125

UK

USA **12.7%**

France **10.2%**

Canada **12.4%**

61
France

25
Switzerland

20
Italy

USA 353

Mexico **19.8%**

Argentina **15.3%**

Brazil **14.6%**

Bolivia **19.5%**

Ethiopia **24.4%**

South Africa **20.6%**

Kenya **23.7%**

KEY

Spending on education
Percentage of government budget spent on education

Nobel Prizes
Number of Nobel laureates

Teacher conditions

Wealthier countries, such as the USA and Finland, spend more on education so they usually have more teachers available than poorer countries, such as Bangladesh.

Number of students per teacher in secondary education

Central African Republic 68.1

Bangladesh 32.2

Dominican Republic 29.2

USA 14.7

China 14.5

France 12.8

Finland 9.3

Cayman Islands 5.3

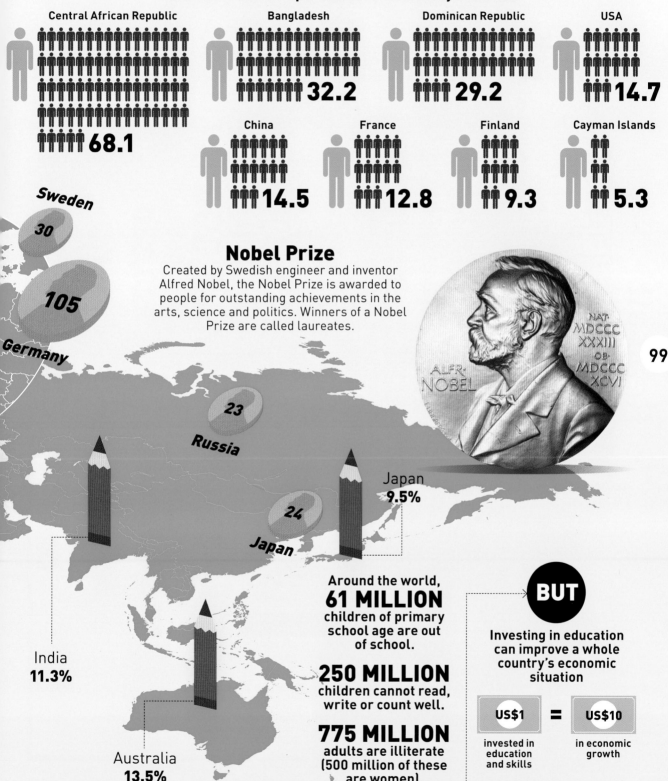

Nobel Prize

Created by Swedish engineer and inventor Alfred Nobel, the Nobel Prize is awarded to people for outstanding achievements in the arts, science and politics. Winners of a Nobel Prize are called laureates.

Sweden 30

Germany 105

Russia 23

Japan 24

Japan 9.5%

India 11.3%

Australia 13.5%

Around the world, **61 MILLION** children of primary school age are out of school.

250 MILLION children cannot read, write or count well.

775 MILLION adults are illiterate (500 million of these are women).

BUT

Investing in education can improve a whole country's economic situation

US$1 invested in education and skills = US$10 in economic growth

Read all
ABOUT IT

More than one million different books are published every year in every language on the planet. While China and the USA publish the most titles, more are released per head of population in the UK than anywhere else, with 2,875 titles published per one million people.

PUBLISHING AROUND THE WORLD

This map shows the countries with the largest publishing markets and how much they earn each year, as well as some of the biggest-selling authors of all time and the number of books they have sold.

— NEW TITLES PUBLISHED BY COUNTRY —

BRAZIL
501,371

CHINA
448,000

UNITED KINGDOM
220,330

FRANCE
98,306

GERMANY
87,134

SPAIN
78,508

JAPAN **76,465**

ITALY **63,922**

TURKEY **50,752**

NETHERLANDS
25,793

RUSSIA
Leo Tolstoy
413 million

SWEDEN
Astrid Lindgren
145 million

USA

22,918 million euros

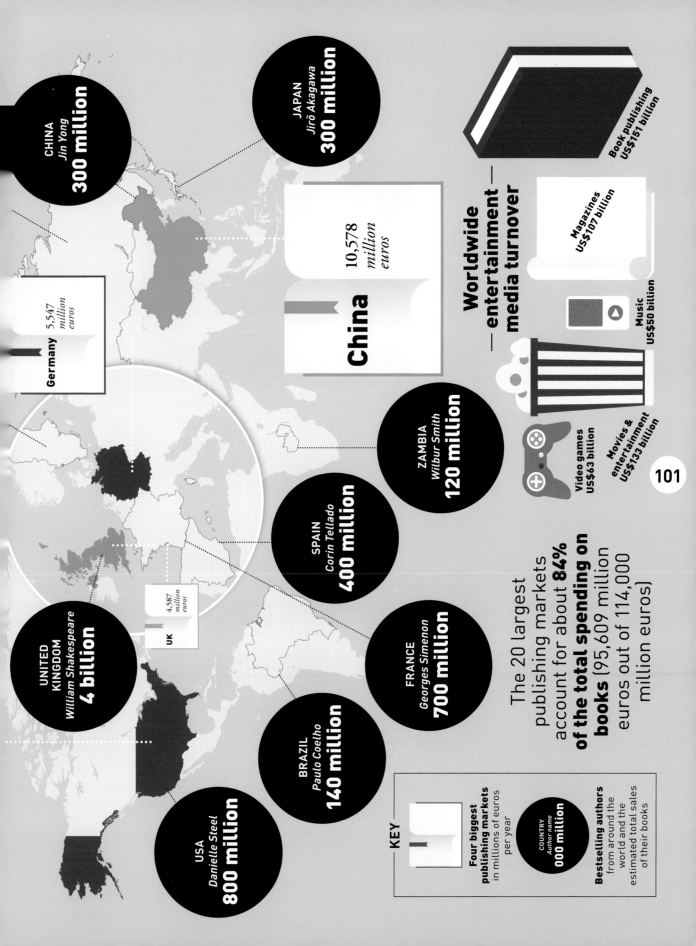

CHINA
Jin Yong
300 million

JAPAN
Jirō Akagawa
300 million

Book publishing
US$151 billion

China

10,578
*million
euros*

Germany
5,547
*million
euros*

**Worldwide
— entertainment —
media turnover**

Magazines
US$107 billion

Music
US$50 billion

Movies &
entertainment
US$133 billion

Video games
US$63 billion

ZAMBIA
Wilbur Smith
120 million

SPAIN
Corin Tellado
400 million

UK
4,587
*million
euros*

UNITED
KINGDOM
William Shakespeare
4 billion

FRANCE
Georges Simenon
700 million

The 20 largest
publishing markets
account for about **84%
of the total spending on
books** (95,609 million
euros out of 114,000
million euros)

BRAZIL
Paulo Coelho
140 million

USA
Danielle Steel
800 million

KEY

**Four biggest
publishing markets**
in millions of euros
per year

COUNTRY
Author name
000 million

Bestselling authors
from around the
world and the
estimated total sales
of their books

101

Education
AND LITERACY

The ability to read and write is the basis of a good education, but levels and abilities vary greatly around the world, depending largely on the wealth of the country. Levels of literacy and education can also vary between men and women, even in the same country.

LITERACY RATES

This map shows the percentages of people who can read and write in countries with some of the highest and lowest rates in the world, as well as the percentages of men and women who are literate.

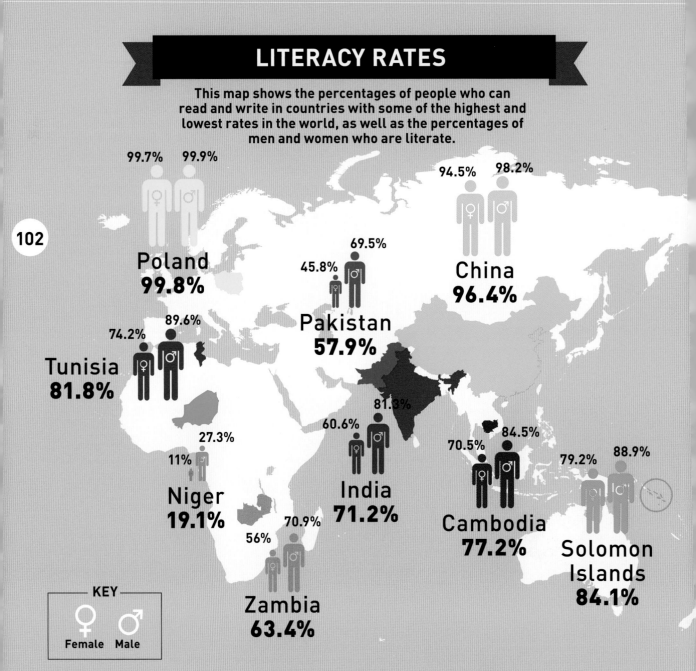

99.7%   99.9%
Poland
99.8%

94.5%   98.2%
China
96.4%

69.5%
45.8%
Pakistan
57.9%

74.2%   89.6%
Tunisia
81.8%

27.3%
11%
Niger
19.1%

81.3%
60.6%
India
71.2%

70.5%   84.5%
Cambodia
77.2%

79.2%   88.9%
Solomon Islands
84.1%

70.9%
56%
Zambia
63.4%

KEY
♀ ♂
Female Male

YEARS SPENT IN EDUCATION

Wealthier countries, such as Australia, usually spend more on their schools, universities and colleges than poorer countries, such as the African country of Niger. As such, people in wealthier countries will spend longer in school, gaining a higher literacy rate and more qualifications.

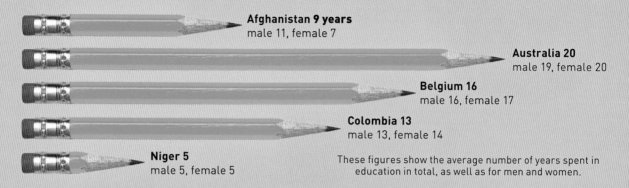

Afghanistan 9 years
male 11, female 7

Australia 20
male 19, female 20

Belgium 16
male 16, female 17

Colombia 13
male 13, female 14

Niger 5
male 5, female 5

These figures show the average number of years spent in education in total, as well as for men and women.

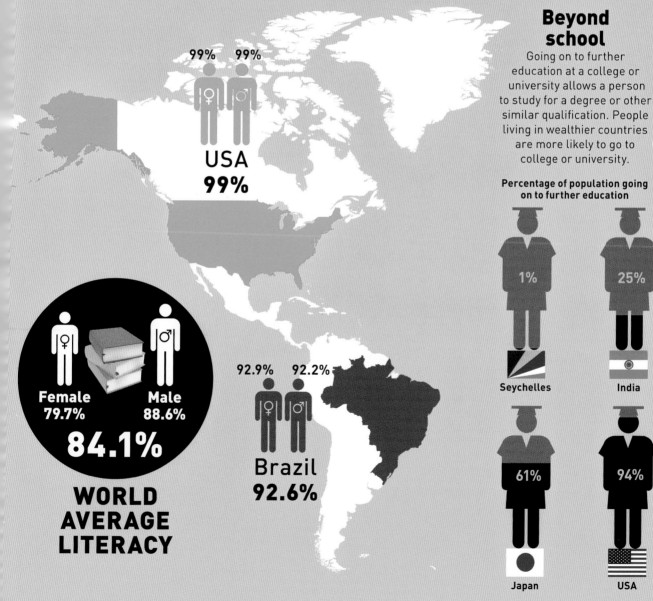

99% 99%

USA
99%

Female 79.7%   **Male 88.6%**

84.1%
WORLD AVERAGE LITERACY

92.9% 92.2%

Brazil
92.6%

Beyond school

Going on to further education at a college or university allows a person to study for a degree or other similar qualification. People living in wealthier countries are more likely to go to college or university.

103

Percentage of population going on to further education

1%
Seychelles

25%
India

61%
Japan

94%
USA

Armed FORCES

The size of a country's armed forces depends on how involved it is in conflicts around the world and its relations with its neighbours. South Korea may be small, but tension with North Korea means that it maintains a large army.

GLOBAL ARMED FORCES

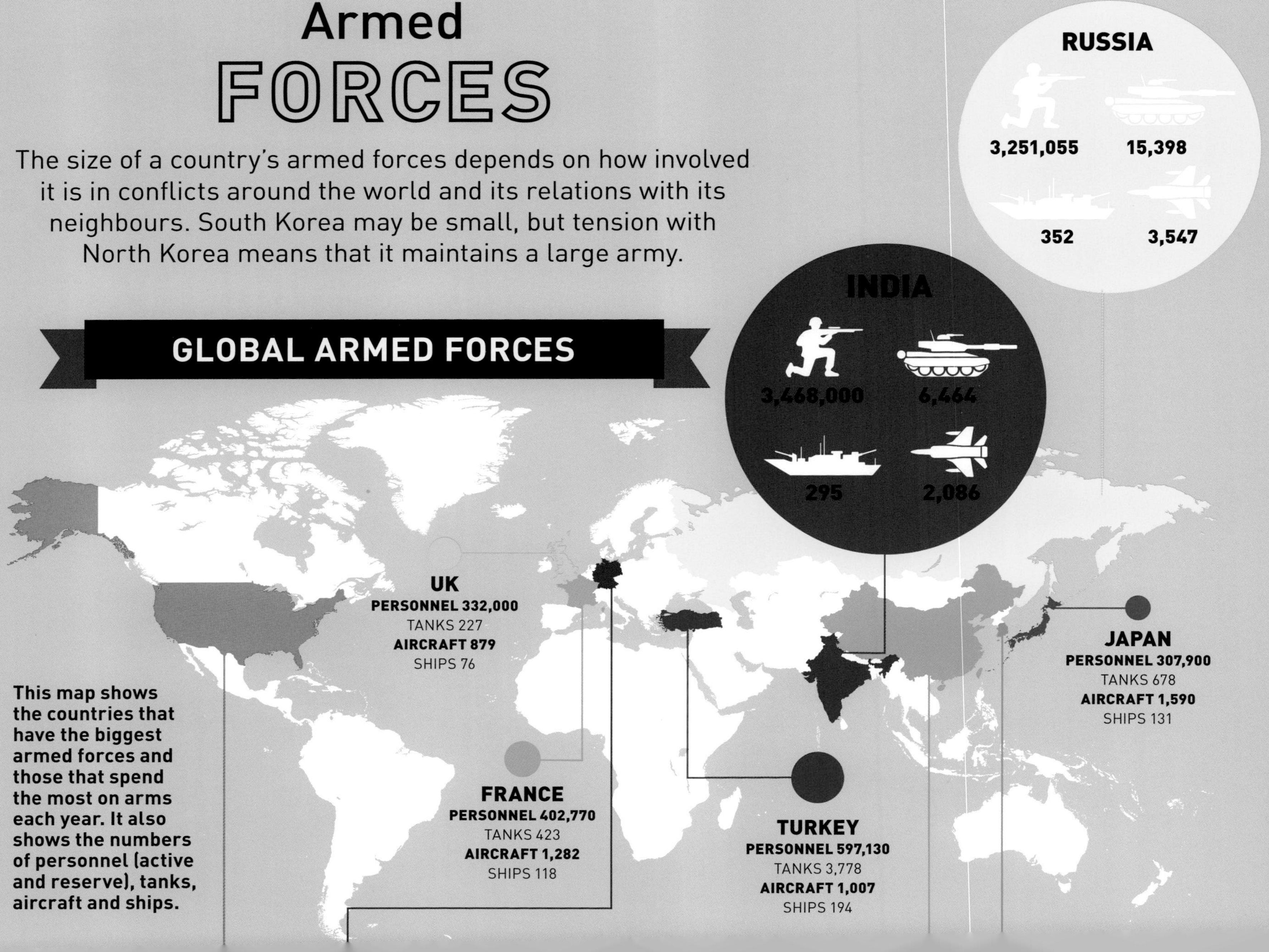

This map shows the countries that have the biggest armed forces and those that spend the most on arms each year. It also shows the numbers of personnel (active and reserve), tanks, aircraft and ships.

RUSSIA

3,251,055

15,398

352

3,547

INDIA

3,468,000

6,464

2,086

295

JAPAN
PERSONNEL 307,900
TANKS 678
AIRCRAFT 1,590
SHIPS 131

TURKEY
PERSONNEL 597,130
TANKS 3,778
AIRCRAFT 1,007
SHIPS 194

UK
PERSONNEL 332,000
TANKS 227
AIRCRAFT 879
SHIPS 76

FRANCE
PERSONNEL 402,770
TANKS 423
AIRCRAFT 1,282
SHIPS 118

SOUTH KOREA

3,525,000

2,381

1,451

166

CHINA

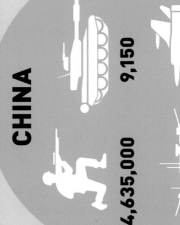

4,635,000

9,150

2,942

714

USA

2,500,000

8,848

13,444

415

GERMANY

PERSONNEL 325,000
TANKS 408
AIRCRAFT 676
SHIPS 81

NUCLEAR POWERS

There are nine countries that have nuclear warheads. While many of these are in storage or waiting to be dismantled, the USA and Russia have about 1,800 that are on constant high-alert status and can be fired at a moment's notice.

= 100 WARHEADS

FRANCE 300
(1.8%)

CHINA 260
(1.6%)

UK 225
(1.4%)

PAKISTAN 120
(0.75%)

INDIA 120
(0.7%)

ISRAEL 80
(0.5%)

NORTH KOREA
FEWER THAN
10 (0.06%)

USA 7,100 (44%)

RUSSIA 7,700 (48% OF GLOBAL NUMBER)

TOTAL: ABOUT 16,000

Space
LAUNCHES

As Earth rotates, its surface moves faster at the equator (about 1,675 km/h) than at the poles (where it moves at 0 km/h). For this reason, many of the sites used to launch rockets into space are found between the two tropics either side of the Equator. Rockets can use the speed of Earth's rotation to give them an extra boost.

LAUNCH SITES

This map shows some of the main launch sites around the world. As well as the USA and Russia, places that are actively involved in launching rockets into space include China, India and Europe. There are also a number of private companies that have built and operate their own rockets.

Kennedy Space Center, USA
Based on the east coast of Florida, USA, the Kennedy Space Center has launched every manned NASA flight, including the Apollo missions to the Moon and the Space Shuttle.

Baikonur, Kazakhstan
The Baikonur Cosmodrome is the world's oldest and biggest space launch site. The first manmade object to orbit Earth, Sputnik 1, and the first human in space, Yuri Gagarin, both blasted off from this facility.

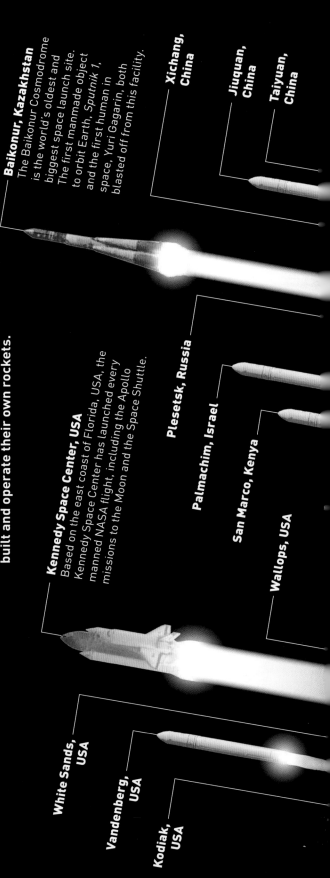

Xichang, China

Jiuquan, China

Taiyuan, China

Plesetsk, Russia

Palmachim, Israel

San Marco, Kenya

Wallops, USA

White Sands, USA

Vandenberg, USA

Kodiak, USA

Svobodny,
Russia

Kagoshima,
Japan

Kwajalein,
Marshall Islands

Sriharikota,
India

Woomera, Australia

Kennedy Space
Center, USA

Alcantara, Brazil

Kourou,
French Guiana

Equator

Landing on Mars

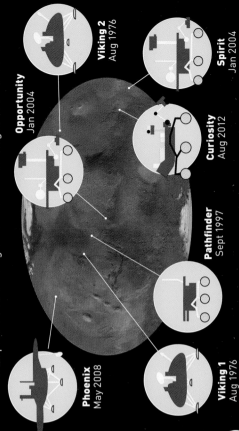

Seven robot spacecraft have successfully landed on the surface of Mars. Of these, four were static landers, while the other four were rovers and able to travel around the Martian surface, studying the rocks and the atmosphere and sending information and images back to Earth.

Viking 2 Aug 1976

Spirit Jan 2004

Opportunity Jan 2004

Curiosity Aug 2012

Pathfinder Sept 1997

Phoenix May 2008

Viking 1 Aug 1976

TO THE MOON

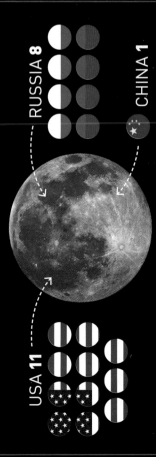

To date, only three countries have successfully launched missions to land on the Moon. Of these 20 missions, only six were manned and just 12 people have actually walked on the lunar surface.

USA **11**

RUSSIA **8**

CHINA **1**

Mapping the
WORLD

The maps in this book are two-dimensional representations of our ballshaped world. Maps allow us to display a huge range of information, including the size of the countries and where people live.

PROJECTIONS

Converting the three-dimensional world into a two-dimensional map can produce different views, called projections. These projections can show different areas of the Earth.

GLOBE
Earth is shaped like a ball, with the landmasses wrapped around it.

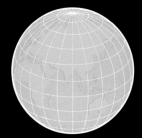

CURVED
Some maps show parts of the world as they would appear on this ball.

FLAT
Maps of the whole world show the landmasses laid out flat. The maps in this book use projections like this.

TYPES OF MAP

Different types of map can show different types of information. Physical maps show physical features, such as mountains and rivers, while political maps show countries and cities. Schematic maps show specific types of information, such as routes on an underground train network, and they may not necessarily show things in exactly the right place.

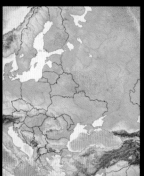

Physical map

Political map

Schematic map

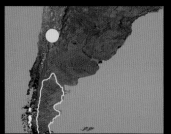

Coloured regions

Scaled symbols

MAP SYMBOLS

Maps use lots of symbols to show information, such as blue lines for rivers and colours for different regions. Some of the symbols in this book show the locations of subjects, or the symbols are different sizes to represent different values – the bigger the symbol, the greater the value.

108

GLOSSARY

ANCESTOR
An individual or a species from which a modern person or species has descended.

BIODIVERSITY
The number and range of different plant and animal species that live in a region.

CALORIE
A unit of energy our bodies get from food. The energy values of different foods are measured in calories. Specifically, a calorie is the amount of energy needed to raise the temperature of 1 g of water by 1°C.

CARNIVAL
An outdoor, public celebration that often takes place before the Christian season of Lent. Lent marks a period of fasting and prayer.

CIVILISATIONS
A society that has reached a high level of social development. For example, it may have invented sophisticated political, legal and writing systems, and created monumental art and architecture.

CLIMATE
The long-term weather conditions that a region experiences. Climate can be affected by how close a region is to the Equator, physical features such as mountains and how close it is to the ocean.

CLIMATE CHANGE
The change in Earth's entire climate, and in specific climates around the world.

CONTINENT
One of seven large land masses that make up Earth's land surface.

CRUDE OIL
Oil that has been pumped out of the ground, before it has been refined into other products, such as petroleum.

CURRENCY
A method of payment for goods and services, usually in the form of paper notes and metal coins, which is accepted in a country or region. It is usually controlled by a government or a central bank.

DEFORESTATION
The clearing of large areas of forest, usually to make way for farms, mines or urban areas.

DESERTIFICATION
When regions become deserts.

DORMANT VOLCANO
A type of volcano that has not erupted for a long period of time, but could still erupt in the future.

DROUGHT
An extended period when very little rain falls.

EMPIRE
A large territory, often including different cultures and peoples, that is united through conquest under the rule of one country.

ENDANGERED
When the numbers of a species have become so low, that it is in danger of becoming extinct.

EQUATOR
The line that runs horizontally around Earth at its widest part.

EXPORT
To move goods and services out of a country.

FAVELA
The Portuguese name given to the enormous shanty towns that grow up in and around major cities throughout Brazil.

FERTILITY RATE
The average number of children that a woman will give birth to in her lifetime.

GROSS DOMESTIC PRODUCT (GDP)
The value of the goods and services that are produced by a country over a year. The GDP can be shown as the total value produced by an entire country over a year or as the average for each person living in that country (per capita).

HIGH-INCOME COUNTRY
According to the World Bank, this is a country where each person earns more than US$12,736 a year on average.

IMPORT
To move goods and services into a country.

INVESTMENT
The money spent on something in the hope that it will provide future benefits or

KILOWATT HOUR (KWH)
A unit used to measure energy being transmitted or used. It is equivalent to 1,000 watts per hour and is used to measure electricity usage.

LAVA
Molten rock that has reached Earth's surface during a volcanic eruption.

LIFE EXPECTANCY
The number of years a person can expect to live for. Life expectancy depends on a number of factors, including where a person lives, whether they are male or female, how long their parents lived for and their lifestyle.

LOW-INCOME COUNTRY
According to the World Bank, this is a country where each person earns less than US$1,045 a year on average.

MARKET
The trading of goods or services in different territories and industries. Usually, the level of supply and demand sets the price of the goods and services traded.

MIGRATION
The movement of animals to a new area, usually in search of food, water, partners to mate with, or a suitable place to raise young.

MINIMUM WAGE
The lowest wage an employer can legally pay a worker. Not all countries have a legal minimum wage.

MONARCHY
A type of government where the head of state is a king or queen.

OBESITY
A medical condition where a person has accumulated so much fat that it threatens his or her health.

PILGRIMAGE
A journey with a spiritual meaning, for example to a place that is important to a person's religious faith, such as a shrine.

PLANTATION
A large piece of land that is being used to grow a single crop, such as the oil palm or sugar cane.

REFORESTATION
The planting of new forests to replace those that have been cut down.

REPUBLIC
A type of government where the population votes in the people who will govern them.

RESPIRATORY
Relating to your breathing system, including the lungs and airways.

SANITATION
The safe disposal of waste, including human waste, and stopping people from coming into contact with that waste.

SMARTPHONE
A type of mobile phone that can send emails, access the internet and run applications, known as apps.

SOCIAL NETWORK
An online forum where users share thoughts, images and music with others.

SPECIES
A group of living organisms that are very similar to each other and can reproduce with each other to produce fertile offspring.

STREAMING
An online stream of multimedia, such as music or a movie, that a user can receive without having to download it to a phone or a computer.

TECTONIC PLATES
The large pieces of Earth's surface that fit together to form the crust. These pieces are crashing into each other, pulling apart or rubbing against one another.

TEU
Short for twenty-foot equivalent unit, it is a unit used to describe how much cargo ships can carry. It refers to the large metal containers that are often stacked on the ships' decks.

TROPICS
The regions on Earth that lie on either side of the equator.

URBANISATION
The rate at which people move from the countryside and into towns and cities.

INDEX

111

112

The publisher would like to thank the following for their kind permission to reproduce their photographs: p5 NASA; p6–7 all istockphoto.com/photokey; p17tl istockphoto.com/Harvepino; p17tr istockphoto.com/robh; p17ct istockphoto.com/RafalBelzowski; p17cr istockphoto.com/jdavidlong; p20–21 istockphoto.com/DRB Images, LLC; p26–27 istockphoto.com/sorbetto, istockphoto.com/Aaltazar, istockphoto.com/drmakkoy, shutterstock/Oktora, Decorwithme | Dreamstime.com; p28–29 istockphoto.com/Zurijeta; p29tr istockphoto.com/leungchopan; p29cr istockphoto.com/Chris Hepburn; p29br istockphoto.com/Xavier Arnau; p32 noun project/Félix Péault; p36–37 NASA; p36–37 light bulbs istockphoto.com/choness; p38bl istockphoto.com/Olena Druzhynina; p41cr istockphoto.com/mikdam; p42–43 palm oil fruit istockphoto.com/nop16; p43l istockphoto.com/yotrak; p43br istockphoto.com/kjorgen; p44br istockphoto.com/Mlenny; p44–45, 8–9, 14–15 NASA; p45tl istockphoto.com/ah_fotobox; p45tc istockphoto.com/Daniel Barnes; p45tr istockphoto.com/lopurice; p45cr istockphoto.com/wcjohnston; p45bl istockphoto.com/KeithBinns; p47r istockphoto.com/vesilvio; p47t istockphoto.com/compassandcamera; p48–49 background istockophoto.com/Keilchihiki; p51tl istockphoto.com/luoman; p51tc istockphoto.com/kikkerdirk; p51tr istockphoto.com/GordonImages; p52bl, 53tl istockphoto.com/Josef Friedhuber; p52tc, 53tr istockphoto.com/MogensTrolle; p52tr, 53clt istockphoto.com/John Carnemolia; p52ct, 53cl istockphoto.com/yoglimogli; p52crt, 53br istockphoto.com/aurigadesign; p52c, 53cr istockphoto.com/ultrapro; p52cr, 53crt istockphoto.com/Guenter Guni; p52cr, 53crb istockphoto.com/WLDavies; p52bc, 53clb NOAA; p52br, 53bl istockphoto/com/hfrankWI; p53tr istockphoto.com/Lucyna Koch; p54tl istockphoto.com/groveb; p54cr istockphoto.com/doescher; p54br istockphoto.com/Gannet77; p54–55c dreamstime.com/Pipa100; p55t shutterstock.com/aquapix; p55ct shutterstock.com/Vishnevskiy Vasily; p55cl istockphoto.com/bbuong; p55cr istockphoto.com/irin717; p55cb istockphoto.com; p56–57 istockphoto.com/tomlamela; p58-59 istockphoto.com/David Sucsy; p59bc istockphoto.com; p59r isotckphoto.com/Pavlo_K; p60–61 istockphoto.com/spanteldotru; p63br istockphoto.com/Carlos_bcn; p65t all istockphoto.com/drewhadley; p66–67 istockphoto.com/Varijanta, istockphoto.com/Askold Romanov; p71br istockphoto.com/Daniel Barnes; p74–75 istockphoto.com/MillefloreImages; p75br istockphoto.com/tavor; p80bc noun project/Creative Stall PK; p83t istockphoto.com/Courtney Keating; p84–85 and 85t istockphoto.com/rypson; p84cr istockphoto.com/W6; p84 cl istockphoto.com/dibrova; p84bl istockphoto.com/WillSelarep; p84br istockphoto.com/Nikada; p85bl istockphoto.com/06photo; p87cr istockphoto.com/luoman; p87tl istockphoto.com/Joel Carillet; p87tr istockphoto.com/Ary6; p87tl istockphoto.com/MaestroBooks; p87tr istockphoto.com/jon11; p87cl istockphoto.com/tamara_kulikova; p87c istockphoto.com/TimEKlein; p87cb istockphoto.com/deadandliving; p87br istockphoto.com/bukharova; p88cr istockphoto.com/Nikada; p89t istockphoto.com/Yoav Peled; p89tl istockphoto.com/afby71; p89tc istockphoto.com/traveler1116; p89c istockphoto.com/oytun karadayi; p89cr istockphoto.com/Rufous52; p91br Dreamstime.com/Taronin; p96tl noun project/Parker Foote; p97t noun project/Maximillian Piras; p97bc noun project/Robert Salazar Jr.; p99cr shutterstock.com/Pe3k; p103t all istockphoto.com/bluestocking; p104–105 istockphoto.com/ozgurartug; p106–107 NASA; p108c istockphoto.com/nicoolay; p108cr istockphoto.com/Manakin.